POISON

To Luke!

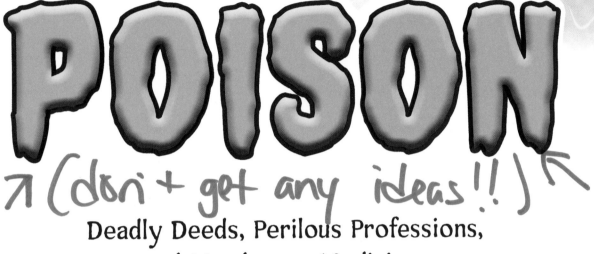

→ (don't get any ideas!!) ↖

Deadly Deeds, Perilous Professions, and Murderous Medicines

♡ Sarah Albee

SARAH ALBEE

CROWN BOOKS
FOR YOUNG READERS

NEW YORK

Library of Congress Cataloging-in-Publication Data
Names: Albee, Sarah, author.
Title: Poison : deadly deeds, perilous professions, and murderous medicines / Sarah Albee.
Description: First edition. | New York : Crown Books for Young Readers, [2017] |
Audience: Ages 8–12. | Audience: Grades 4–6.
Identifiers: LCCN 2016009205 | ISBN 978-1-101-93223-0 (pb) | ISBN 978-1-101-93224-7 (glb) |
ISBN 978-1-101-93225-4 (epub)
Subjects: LCSH: Poisons—Juvenile literature. | Toxicology—Juvenile literature. | Poisoning—Juvenile
literature. | Poisons—History—Juvenile literature. | Hazardous substances—Juvenile literature.
Classification: LCC RA1214.A43 2017 | DDC 615.9—dc23

MANUFACTURED IN CHINA
10 9 8 7 6 5 4 3 2 1
First Edition

For Jon, as ever

CONTENTS

AUTHOR'S NOTE

Let's get one thing straight, right off the bat: this is not a how-to book. It's a history book. It's about how people have poisoned one another from ancient times to the present.

Why did I write this book? When I was a kid, I was fascinated by stories that involved poison. And I wondered, did poisons like these exist in real life? I moved from *Snow White* and *Sleeping Beauty* to Sherlock Holmes and Agatha Christie mysteries, and then, in college, I fell hard for Shakespeare, whose plays are awash in poison. (I know, he can be tough going in middle school, but trust me on this one.) And now, because I have the world's best job as a nonfiction writer, and the world's best editor, who wants to publish what I write, I have been able to research and write about the poisons that have fascinated me my whole life, to find out where they come from, how they work, and who may have been poisoned by them.

What's not in this book? Except for a few passing references, I made the decision not to include genocidal maniacs, serial killers, run-of-the-mill murder cases, or poisons used by evil rulers in warfare or in concentration camps. There are other books about these awful people and terrible events, if you are curious to read further. Other things that didn't make the cut: industrial accidents, chemical disasters, air pollution, and accidental poisonings by venomous animals and toxic plants. And, as much as I'd love to have included famous poisonings in literature, the book would have been five thousand pages longer, and my editor would probably have poisoned me herself. (Because she certainly knows how, at this point.)

Also, this book is by no means a comprehensive study of all the poisons in the world. Because I come from a Western culture and speak English, there's an emphasis on stories about poisons and poisonings from Western Europe, England, and America. I don't mean to suggest that fascinating poisonings haven't happened in the rest of the world. But I was limited by language barriers and by the oral tradition of many cultures (that is, a history spoken rather than written down), which makes it doubly difficult for a researcher to dig up firm facts. I hope you'll be inspired to look up some of these stories yourself.

1

BAD SOLUTIONS

An Introduction to Poisons

Poison is in everything, and no thing is without poison.
The dosage makes it either a poison or a remedy.
—Paracelsus

POISONS AND POISONERS

Look up. Notice anything funny going on? Are people eyeing you strangely? Have they nudged their lunch trays a little farther away from you?

Maybe it's because you're reading a book about poison.

Even in this day and age, with tamper-proof packaging and antibiotics and FDA regulations, the whole notion of poison still creeps people out.

What is it about poison that both fascinates and horrifies us? Maybe it's that murder by poison is the ultimate premeditated crime. To poison someone on purpose requires plotting. You

Poisons—they're not just the stuff of fairy tales.

have to plan the deed, purchase the poison, and secretly slip it into your victim's food or drink. Then you bide your time and wait for the poison to take effect.

Yes, poisoners are pernicious.

Also, it's hard for us to grasp how poison actually works, deep down at the molecular level. How could a dust-sized fleck of polonium-210 cause a person to vomit uncontrollably, turn yellow, lose all his hair, emit radioactive particles, and then die in agony? No wonder people in the old days thought poison was magic, or the work of the devil, or the revenge of angry gods.

Humans have been poisoning one another for more than six thousand years. Poison is part of our culture, an endless source of fascination for novelists, playwrights, and historians. It's the dark side of our dark side.

DARK DEEDS

As recently as the early twentieth century, poison was usually freely available. Anyone could walk into a drugstore and buy heroin, opium, arsenic, or strychnine. Even a glass of Coca-Cola came with a jolt of cocaine to wash down your lunch.

Back when it was easy to find poison and easy to get away with it, poisoning an enemy was a convenient way to remove an obstacle in your path to power, or to an inheritance. Sitting on a throne could be an extreme sport. Before divorce was legal or socially acceptable, people with inconvenient spouses sometimes turned to poison because they saw it as the only way out of a problematic marriage.

Ruthless rulers in history could never quite trust their frenemies.

In the days before scientists knew how to test for poison, a lot of poisoners got away with murder, and many innocent people were accused of crimes they hadn't committed. When someone died quickly, poison rumors swirled. Yet the skilled poisoners didn't get caught, because their victims' symptoms often imitated those of actual illnesses. Which makes it doubly difficult for those of us living now to know for sure if someone who lived a long time ago was killed by poison or died of natural causes. You can draw your own conclusions in the Poisoned or Not? boxes throughout the book.

NOT SO FAST

We've all seen movies in which someone takes a sip from a cup, clutches his throat, rolls his eyes upward, and keels over dead. But in real life, poison seldom works that way. There aren't that many poisons that can kill you within seconds. More often, the process of being poisoned is slow and agonizing. Over time, different kinds of poisons might cause people to stagger

Poisoning is an ugly business. Actual poison victims rarely looked this good.

drunkenly, glow in the dark, or turn bright blue. And death by poison is almost never Hollywood pretty. Some poisons cause victims to drool, vomit blood, spasm violently, or twitch all over. Others turn them into two-ended fountains of uncontrolled vomiting and diarrhea. Even the fastest-acting poisons can cause extreme pain and suffering before the victim dies.

DOCTORS WITHOUT ORDERS

The history of poison is also the history of medicine. In the past, doctors turned to deadly poisons to try to heal their patients because the poisonous chemicals *did* stuff

to the human body. Poisons could make people see things that weren't there, babble, drool, convulse, and dance. Physicians reasoned that patients suffering from an extreme disease should be treated with an extreme medicine—which is sort of the idea behind modern chemotherapy. Poisons used as medicine made patients poop, tremble, barf, sweat, and sleep. A toxic substance that could block your nerves from sending signals to the brain could blunt the pain of an operation and, with luck, not kill you in the process. Sometimes it even made you feel better.

Step right up! Get your antidote, known as a theriac, before it's too late. An antidote is something that counteracts the effects of a poison.

DON'T TRY THIS AT HOME

Sorry to disappoint you, but we're not going to teach you how to extract the poison from that potted plant on your patio, or how to plan the perfect, undetectable murder.

Not to worry, though. There will be plenty of nasty stories, several unsolved mysteries, and even some famous cases when the poison detectives caught the poisoners. There should be something to please everyone, from true-crime fans to history buffs to science geeks.

Poison maker or forensic scientist? You can't tell the good guys from the bad guys just by sight in this book.

MODERN-DAY POISONS

As a murder weapon, poison has mostly gone out of fashion. It's now too easy to get caught. Over the past 150 years, scientists have figured out how to test for poison in a

living person and to identify poison in a dead one. This type of science is called forensic toxicology, and you can read more about that in chapter eight (see Blood, Sweat, and Smears, p. 99). But old-school poisoners have been replaced by more modern ones, different but equally evil.

This book is about the battle between poisoners and the people trying to stop them. It's about the power of science—how it can kill us and save our lives. It's about poisons that have resulted from human activity—poisons that people have encountered on the job, in the environment, and in their homes. It's about the history of medicine and the rise of the public health movement. We'll learn about the role poisons have played in history, science, religion, slavery, medicine, industry, jobs, advertising, and everyday life. Because as long as humans have lived in social groups, poisons have played a part.

LET'S GET THIS STRAIGHT: DEFINING POISON

Over the past four thousand years, humans have learned how to extract poisonous elements from the earth and to collect toxic chemicals from plants and animals, and have used them as drugs, medicines, and murder weapons. Where did they find them?

Criminal Elements

Some poisons are found naturally in the earth's crust, in the form of elements. These include mercury, arsenic, antimony, lead, thallium, radium, and polonium.

WHAT'S AN ELEMENT?

Everything is made of elements. The food you eat, the water you drink, the clothes you wear, your pet hamster, and you are all made of elements. There are 118 elements that we know of. One single unit of an element is called an atom.

When atoms bond with one another, they form a molecule. If at least two of the atoms are different elements, you also have a chemical compound. (Check the glossary for a more technical definition of an element.)

PERIODIC TABLE OF THE ELEMENTS

1 H 1.0079 Hydrogen																	2 He 4.0026 Helium
3 Li 6.941 Lithium	4 Be 9.0122 Beryllium											5 B 10.811 Boron	6 C 12.011 Carbon	7 N 14.007 Nitrogen	8 O 15.999 Oxygen	9 F 18.998 Fluorine	10 Ne 20.180 Neon
11 Na 22.990 Sodium	12 Mg 24.305 Magnesium											13 Al 26.982 Aluminium	14 Si 28.086 Silicon	15 P 30.974 Phosphorus	16 S 32.065 Sulfur	17 Cl 35.453 Chlorine	18 Ar 39.948 Argon
19 K 39.098 Potassium	20 Ca 40.078 Calcium	21 Sc 44.956 Scandium	22 Ti 47.867 Titanium	23 V 50.942 Vanadium	24 Cr 51.996 Chromium	25 Mn 54.938 Manganese	26 Fe 55.845 Iron	27 Co 58.933 Cobalt	28 Ni 58.693 Nickel	29 Cu 63.546 Copper	30 Zn 65.39 Zinc	31 Ga 69.723 Gallium	32 Ge 72.64 Germanium	33 As 74.992 Arsenic	34 Se 78.96 Selenium	35 Br 79.904 Bromine	36 Kr 83.80 Krypton
37 Rb 85.468 Rubidium	38 Sr 87.62 Strontium	39 Y 88.906 Yttrium	40 Zr 91.224 Zirconium	41 Nb 92.906 Niobium	42 Mo 95.94 Molybdenum	43 Tc 98.906 Technetium	44 Ru 101.07 Ruthenium	45 Rh 102.91 Rhodium	46 Pd 106.42 Palladium	47 Ag 107.87 Silver	48 Cd 112.41 Cadmium	49 In 114.82 Indium	50 Sn 118.71 Tin	51 Sb 121.76 Antimony	52 Te 127.60 Tellurium	53 I 126.90 Iodine	54 Xe 131.29 Xenon
55 Cs 132.91 Cesium	56 Ba 137.33 Barium	57 - 71 La-Lu	72 Hf 178.49 Hafnium	73 Ta 180.95 Tantalum	74 W 183.84 Tungsten	75 Re 186.21 Rhenium	76 Os 190.23 Osmium	77 Ir 192.22 Iridium	78 Pt 195.05 Platinum	79 Au 196.97 Gold	80 Hg 200.50 Mercury	81 Tl 204.38 Thallium	82 Pb 207.2 Lead	83 Bi 208.98 Bismuth	84 Po 209 Polonium	85 At 210 Astatine	86 Rn 222 Radon
87 Fr 223 Francium	88 Ra 226 Radium	89 - 103 Ac-Lr	104 Rf 261 Rutherfordium	105 Db 262 Dubnium	106 Sg 266 Seaborgium	107 Bh 264 Bohrium	108 Hs 269 Hassium	109 Mt 268 Meitnerium	110 Uun 269 Ununnilium	111 Uuu 272 Unununium	112 Uub 1.0079 Ununbium	113 Uut Ununtrium	114 Uuq 289 Ununquadium	115 Uup 288 Ununpentium	116 Uuh Ununhexium	117 Uus Ununseptium	118 Uuo Ununoctium

Lanthanide series	57 La 138.91 Lanthanum	58 Ce 140.12 Cerium	59 Pr 140.91 Praseodymium	60 Nd 144.24 Neodymium	61 Pm 145 Promethium	62 Sm 150.36 Samarium	63 Eu 151.90 Europium	64 Gd 157.25 Gadolinium	65 Tb 158.93 Terbium	66 Dy 162.5 Dysprosium	67 Ho 164.90 Holmium	68 Er 1.0079 Erbium	69 Tm 168.93 Thulium	70 Yb 173.04 Ytterbium	71 Lu 1.0079 Lutetium
Actinide series	89 Ac 227 Actinide	90 Th 232.04 Thorium	91 Pa 231.04 Protactinium	92 U 238.03 Uranium	93 Np 237 Neptunium	94 Pu 244 Plutonium	95 Am 243 Americium	96 Cm 247 Curium	97 Bk 247 Berkelium	98 Cf 251 Californium	99 Es 252 Einsteinium	100 Fm 257 Fermium	101 Md 258 Mendelevium	102 No 259 Nobelium	103 Lr 1.0079 Lawrencium

The periodic table includes some extremely poisonous elements. You'll be seeing a lot of them in this book.

Alarming Animals

Some poisons (more correctly known as venoms) are produced by animals. These animals include bees, snakes, poison-dart frogs, and scorpions, among others. Venoms are usually not very toxic if you swallow them but can be deadly if injected into your bloodstream—or if you get bitten or stung.

Do not pet.

Pernicious Plants

Some poisons are produced by plants, usually to defend themselves from being eaten by insects and grazing animals. Plant-produced poisons include strychnine, cocaine, opium, nicotine, and aconite. Scientists call these naturally occurring chemical compounds alkaloids.

Opium, and some prescription pain relievers, come from poppy plants.

So do the poppy seeds on your bagel—without the drug effect.

The Properties of Poisons

A poison is something that causes injury, illness, or death by some sort of chemical change. Practically anything can kill you if you ingest enough of it—you can actually die of too much water, too much salt, or too much sugar. But a classic poison is something that is toxic *at low doses* and that causes illness or an unnatural death by interfering with your body's natural biological processes.

What's the Matter?

Poisons can exist in the form of a solid, a liquid, or a gas. There are four ways a poison can enter your body: you can breathe it in, swallow it, absorb it through your skin, or have it injected directly into your blood.

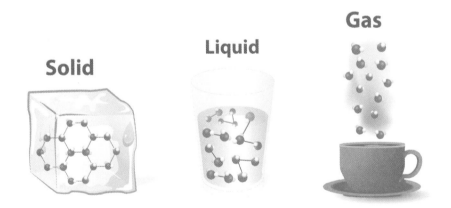

Poison is poison, no MATTER what state it's in.

Once a poison has entered your body, it can mess up a lot of things at the cellular level. Depending on the type, dose, and method of delivery, a victim can sicken gradually over the course of several days or weeks, or can drop dead seconds after being poisoned. What's especially unnerving about poison is that its victim can appear fine

on the outside. But inside, billions of chemical bonds are being created or destroyed, sometimes very rapidly.

For specifics about how each poison works and where each one comes from, you can read the Tox Boxes throughout the book.

THE -*INS* AND -*ANTS* OF TOXINS

Toxicology is the study of poison. A **toxin** is a poisonous chemical produced by plants, animals, or microorganisms. A **toxicant** is a poison that is either human-made or a result of human activity. But for the purposes of this book, we'll say that "toxic" and "poisonous" mean the same thing.

NO BANE, NO GAIN

Poisons in the Ancient World

They put arsenic in his meat
And stared aghast to watch him eat;
They poured strychnine in his cup
And shook to see him drink it up.
—A. E. Housman on Mithridates

PREHISTORIC POISONS

Probably the first humans to use poison lived in modern-day South Africa about twenty-four thousand years ago. They hunted with pointed sticks that archaeologists believe were treated with poison. The poison may have come from the castor-oil plant. But they were not the only people to have this idea. In France, archaeologists found ancient spearheads and arrowheads dating slightly later, with little indentations that may have held poison.

It was only a matter of time before someone realized you could slip some into your enemy's stew pot.

Has anyone seen my poison arrow?

9

OH MY GODDESS

Accidental and job-related poisonings seemed to occur frequently in the ancient world. But the Sumerians (who lived around 4500 BCE) may have been the first civilization in which people used poison upon one another. They worshipped Gula, a goddess of poisons, who was also the goddess of charms and spells.

THE PITS

The ancient Egyptians were familiar with a variety of poisons. They may also have been the first people with a recorded history of preparing a poison for punishment purposes. According to some translations, an ancient papyrus mentions the "penalty of the peach" as a punishment for uttering God's name out loud. The poison was probably made from crushed peach pits, which contain a form of cyanide.

Name: Cyanide [SY-uh-nyde]

Other names: Prussic acid, hydrogen cyanide, potassium cyanide

Source: Many plants contain cyanide compounds, including the leaves of the yew tree, the leaves of the cherry laurel, and the pits and seeds of apricots, cherries, bitter almonds, apples, and peaches, as well as the roots of the cassava plant.

How it's delivered: Swallowed in powder or liquid form, or breathed in as a gas

Effects: Cyanide kills rapidly but horribly. Victims may gasp desperately for air before they suffocate to death. The time between the dose and symptoms showing up can be as short as ten seconds, depending on how pure the cyanide is and how much the victim takes in. Smaller doses cause dizziness, trouble breathing, and loss of consciousness. Sometimes the dead body gives off a faint smell of almonds.

MOISTURIZED TO DEATH?

In 2009, a plain bottle in the collection of the Egyptian Museum in Bonn, Germany, caught the eye of the curator. It had belonged to the Egyptian queen Hatshepsut (ca. 1450 BCE) and had long been thought to be a perfume bottle. It was sealed with the original clay stopper. Did it still contain any of the original contents? he wondered. After a chemical analysis, scientists found traces of palm oil, some other stuff used to treat skin diseases, and, most important, a poisonous substance called benzopyrene. So it wasn't a perfume after all. The bottle appears to have contained a medicated skin lotion. Egyptologists have long known that chronic skin problems, including eczema, ran in Queen Hatshepsut's family. Could slathering herself with the poisonous skin cream have led to her death?

Does my face look dry to you?

ANCIENT EGYPTIAN MAKEUP—GET THE LOOK!

Whether you're male or female, pharaoh or slave, don't even think of stepping out without your makeup on and your hair or wig oiled to a shine. You can outline your eyes with a black paste called kohl, made of soot, animal fat, and antimony (see Tox Box, p. 43). Green eye shadow is made from malachite (a green copper ore) or galena (a lead-based color).

Dreadful detail: in King Tut's tomb they found tubes of orpiment and realgar—arsenic-based cosmetics. Because compounds of arsenic and lead (see Tox Boxes, pp. 13 and 23) come in excellent colors and are easy to grind into a powder, they were used frequently for makeup. Regular use would have caused serious skin problems, and even death in the long run.

Looking good
for eternity.

DROP-DEAD GORGEOUS

POISON

Name: Arsenic [AHR-suh-nik]

Other names: Realgar (ruby red), orpiment (intense yellow), inheritance powder

Source: Arsenic is a grayish metallic element found naturally in soil, water, and air. Realgar and orpiment are naturally occurring, brightly colored arsenic compounds that have been used as paints and cosmetics. The deadly white powdered poison popularly used as a murder weapon is a compound known as arsenic trioxide.

Popular poisonous products: Arsenic was a major ingredient in Fowler's Solution (see pp. 104–105). It was also used as a cosmetic, a rodent killer, and an insecticide.

How it's delivered: Swallowed, breathed in, or absorbed through the skin

Effects: Ongoing exposure causes swelling of the face and eyelids, skin sores, loss of appetite, stomach problems, diarrhea, and general ill health. Higher doses may lead to shock, heart and breathing problems, skin cancer, and death.

CH'IN UP

Ch'in (or Qin) Shi Huang (260–210 BCE) proclaimed himself the first emperor of China in 221 BCE. "Mercurial" sums him up rather nicely, and on several levels.

Was he a terrible tyrant, or has history been unkind to him? He did unify China, and he passed some important reforms. He built a lot of highways and canals and, most famously, began building the Great Wall to keep out "barbarians." On the flip side, millions of people were forced to help with all that construction, and many died doing so. He ordered intellectuals to be killed or forced them to become construction workers, and he banned books because he thought knowledgeable people could be dangerous.

A mercurial monarch.

He was also paranoid about poison and terrified of death. He drank mercury regularly, believing it would counter the effects of poison (see Tox Box, p. 15). He sent "magicians" throughout Asia to find the legendary islands of immortality. He employed hundreds of alchemists (see The Birth of Alchemy, pp. 23–24) to create the elixir of life—a formula that would have made him immortal. When some scholars criticized

Qin's life-sized action figures.

his projects, he had 460 of them buried alive. He also forced 750,000 workers to build him a palace for the afterlife, guarded by clay soldiers and surrounded by rivers of liquid mercury.

Eleven years into his reign, he died suddenly of what may have been a mercury overdose while on a road trip through his empire. Four years after his death, his empire collapsed.

Today he is most famous for that elaborate tomb, which was discovered in 1974 by some peasants digging a well. Thousands of life-sized terra-cotta warriors have been uncovered, though much remains to be excavated.

Name: Mercury [MER-kyur-ee]

Source: Mercury is a metallic element. It's found in the earth's crust in combination with other elements—most often in the mineral called cinnabar. It's the only metal that is liquid at room temperature.

Popular poisonous products: Old-fashioned medicines containing mercury included calomel, corrosive sublimate, Dr. Rush's Bilious Pills, and Mercurochrome.

How it's delivered: Swallowed, breathed in, or absorbed through the skin. Most mercury-containing compounds are somewhat toxic if swallowed but extremely toxic if vapors are breathed in.

Effects: Swollen mouth and gums, excess drooling (salivation), loose teeth, bleeding stomach ulcers, personality changes, tremors, a staggering walk, and death. Mercury accumulates in the body over time.

FOOD TASTER

Back in the days when food preparation could be risky (let's start with no refrigerators), it was sometimes hard to know if the meal that made you sick had been poisoned on purpose or by accident. Evil tyrants who survived stomach ailments had little way of knowing whether someone was trying to kill them or if they had eaten a bad oyster. So they often employed food tasters. Food tasters were supposed to protect their boss from both the accidental and on-purpose kinds of poisoning.

Tasting for poison goes back to the ancient Egyptians and continued for centuries. But only rarely can poisons in your food or drink kill you within seconds. Cyanide works quickly, and arsenic and strychnine might make you vomit after a few hours, but even in large doses, the poisons would take at least twenty-four hours to kill someone. By that time, both you and your boss would be long past lunch, so you wouldn't realize who—or what—had poisoned you. Being a food taster was one of the more high-stress jobs of the ancient world, although at least you ate pretty well.

Food fright!

THAT'S CLASSIC

Poison in Ancient Greece and Rome

In every tyrant's heart there springs in the end
This poison, that he cannot trust a friend.
—Aeschylus

TOXIC PLOTS, POISON POTS, AND SHIPBOARD SHOTS

The Greeks and Romans knew a lot about plants and minerals that could both kill and heal. And they didn't hesitate to put that knowledge to use by waging war with toxic tactics against their neighbors. The Athenians accused the Spartans of poisoning their wells. The Carthaginians launched terra-cotta pots filled with deadly stinging scorpions onto the decks of Roman ships. In the seventh century CE, the Byzantines (from the Eastern Roman Empire) concocted a secret and terrifying weapon that became known as Greek fire. The burning liquid could be launched from tubes mounted on the front of ships and was impossible to extinguish. Throwing water on it only made it burn faster and hotter. The formula was so carefully guarded, even the Byzantines lost track of it, but it may have contained some combination of naphtha, sulfur, arsenic, antimony, resin, and pitch.

The ancient Greeks and Romans were the first to use poison in warfare, but sadly, they would not be the last.

Greek fire: the nightmare version of trick birthday candles.

GRECIAN FORMULAS

If you've read some Greek mythology, you know that it is full of tales about poisons. Hercules is given a shirt poisoned with centaur blood. A jealous Medea sends her rival a poisoned dress. Theseus almost drinks a cup of poisoned wine. The Greeks

Hercules— his wardrobe killed.

worshipped many gods and goddesses, and ancient Greek writers tended to blur the line between fiction and fact. (Remember: they believed their gods and goddesses were real.) Still, one thing ancient Greek texts can tell us for sure is that the Greeks knew a lot about poisons.

The Greeks also produced several great physicians. Hippocrates (460–377 BCE) is now generally considered the father of early medicine. Although he got a lot wrong, he was the first to

Modern physicians take the Hippocratic oath, which states how doctors promise to treat their patients.

say that the causes of diseases were natural and not the result of magic. He relied on his own observations and believed that environmental factors could actually be the cause of some ailments. He also believed that extreme diseases called for extreme remedies.

Notable Greek physicians who followed him began to put poisons into categories: animal, vegetable, or mineral (that is, a person could be poisoned by a venomous snake, a toxic plant, or a poisonous metal). They also wrote about antidotes—drugs to counteract a poison's effects. In the second century CE, the Greek physician Galen would write about poisons that could be used as medicine.

For about fourteen hundred years, the works of Hippocrates and Galen would form the foundation of Western medicine. There were positives and negatives to this.

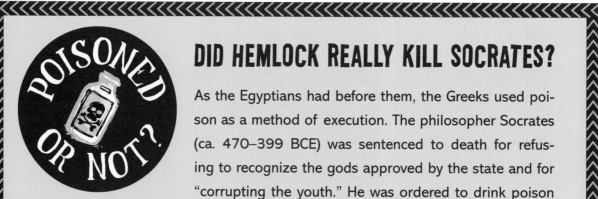

DID HEMLOCK REALLY KILL SOCRATES?

As the Egyptians had before them, the Greeks used poison as a method of execution. The philosopher Socrates (ca. 470–399 BCE) was sentenced to death for refusing to recognize the gods approved by the state and for "corrupting the youth." He was ordered to drink poison hemlock (see Tox Box, p. 21). According to an eyewitness account written by Plato, another famous Greek philosopher, Socrates's death was a gentle one, and he was surrounded by his devoted followers. After drinking the poison, his feet went numb, and the paralysis (numbness) slowly crept upward. "His legs grew cold and stiff," Plato wrote, and after that, his respiratory muscles became paralyzed. His mind remained clear to the end, though. His last words were "Crio, we owe Asklepias a rooster. Pay the debt and do not forget it."

There's no question that Socrates died of poison. The question is, which poison? Historians over the centuries have debated whether Plato's description was accurate. Some have suggested that the symptoms of hemlock poisoning would

Bad to the last drop!

have been far less peaceful. The debate centers around the correct translation of Plato's words; also, what was the exact *type* of hemlock Socrates swallowed? Certain species of hemlock would cause a person to convulse and thrash, and Plato is unhelpful on that front, describing what Socrates drank only as "the drug."

The debate about the poison that killed Socrates was reignited by an incident in 1845 CE. A Scottish tailor named Duncan Gow died after eating a sandwich made for him by his children. They thought it was wild parsley. It turned out to be poison hemlock (which looks like parsley). His symptoms—gradual numbing first of the lower limbs and then the arms, and then a paralysis of his whole body until his breathing stopped—sound remarkably similar to those in Plato's account of Socrates's death. As had been the case with Socrates (according to Plato), Duncan Gow's mind remained clear to the end. So it seems Plato's account may have been medically accurate.

TOX BOX

Name: Poison hemlock

Other names: *Conium maculatum*, poison parsley, devil's porridge

Source: The plant grows wild in many regions around the world, often near streams and ditches and along the sides of the road.

How it's delivered: All parts of the plant are poisonous to humans (and to grazing animals) if swallowed.

Effects: Difficulty breathing, numbness, and death

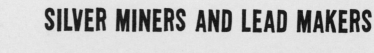

Nice work if you can survive it

SILVER MINERS AND LEAD MAKERS

Mining has always been dangerous. Possibly the worst job in ancient Greece was to be a slave working in the silver mines. Naked slaves were chained to one another in near-total darkness, three hundred feet underground. Lamps burning animal fat might have cast a dim, smoky light. Sometimes miners wouldn't see daylight for weeks. Those who managed not to die of exhaustion would die of lead poisoning (see Tox Box, p. 23) after a few years. (Lead is a by-product of silver mining.)

The lead from the silver mines did not get discarded. It was made into white powdered lead and was used for all sorts of things, including makeup and paint. The process of making it remained unchanged for centuries. Workers buried strips of lead metal in horse poop and doused them with acetic acid. As the smelly mixture sat and fermented, white crystals formed on the metal. Workers scraped the lead crystals off by hand, exposing themselves to toxic lead over time.

The silver mines—very, very poor job-satisfaction ratings.

Name: Lead [led]

Source: Lead is an element with the chemical symbol Pb, from the Latin word *plumbum* ("waterworks"). Lead compounds are found naturally in the earth's crust, often in the mineral called cerussite.

Popular poisonous products: In the sixteenth century, the white-lead cosmetic often used as a skin lightener was called ceruse. In the twentieth century, lead was added to paints and gasoline.

How it's delivered: Swallowed, breathed in, or absorbed through the skin. It moves into the bloodstream and is absorbed into the bones and hair.

Effects: Chronic exposure can cause headaches, depression, hallucinations, difficulty sleeping, a metallic taste in the mouth, abdominal pain, convulsions, paralysis (numbness) of the arms and legs, and problems with the central nervous system. One of the long-term effects is impaired learning ability. Heavy exposure can lead to hallucinations, blindness, coma, and death.

THE GOLD AGE

The Birth of Alchemy

Nearly all societies throughout history have valued gold, and the ancient Greeks were no exception. They thought there were only four elements: earth, air, fire, and water. They didn't realize that gold is an element. They thought you could make it from a

"lesser" metal—all you had to do was figure out how to remove a little air or add a dash of water, or fire, or earth.

The Greeks also believed in wizards and sorcery and astrology and prophets—as would most people for the next thousand or so years. The combination of wanting to make gold and believing in magic led to the creation of the pseudoscience of alchemy, although it wasn't yet called alchemy. It was a combination of science, astrology, and magic. The goal of the alchemists was to change ordinary metals into gold.

Zooming ahead a few centuries: Constantine, the emperor of Constantinople (modern-day Istanbul), decreed in 330 CE that Christianity was the official religion of the Roman Empire. He also outlawed pagan (non-Christian) philosophies—which made what the early alchemists were doing illegal. But manuscripts were smuggled out of Christian Byzantium, relocated, translated, and rediscovered a few centuries later by Arab scholars, who gave alchemy its name. They passed along two core goals that would later be central to European alchemy. The first was to discover the philosopher's stone (which had the power to turn lesser metals into gold). The second was to create the elixir of life (in other words, figure out a way to make a person live forever).

Nowadays the whole idea of changing a base metal into gold sounds silly and completely impossible (and it is). But some of the world's greatest scientists spent time practicing alchemy—including Sir Isaac Newton (see Nice Work: Scientist, pp. 124–125). And some alchemists actually discovered practical chemical procedures for producing dyes, medicines, and poisons.

Oh, Honey, Don't!

In 401 BCE, the ten-thousand-man Greek army, led by its general, Xenophon, was heading back to Greece from a battle with Persia when the weary men pitched camp in a lovely place called Trabzon, along the Black

Sea. There they feasted on wild honey, which was abundant in the area. Soon after, the men staggered around and collapsed by the thousands with dizziness, nausea, blurred vision, and, finally, an almost entire loss of muscle control. The army had been poisoned by the toxic honey, which had been made by bees collecting nectar from rhododendron blossoms, which are poisonous to humans.

The men were sick for several days but finally managed to recover enough to continue their march back to Greece.

MISTRUST BUSTER

There are several versions of a story about the Macedonian king and conqueror Alexander the Great and his physician Philip. An ill Alexander was about to drink down some medicine, prepared by Philip, when he received a note warning him that the physician had been bribed and planned to poison him. Alexander handed the note to Philip as he drank down the medicine, to show his trust in the man. (He recovered.)

Read it and weep.

THE DAILY GRIND

Mithridates VI (120–63 BCE)—his name was pronounced *mith-rih-DAY-teez*—was king of Pontus, which is part of modern-day Turkey. He was also the sworn enemy of Rome.

He was so afraid of being poisoned that he regularly took small doses of different poisons in an attempt to develop immunity. He even had toxic chemicals fed to ducks and drank their blood. He regularly tested his poisons and antidotes on slaves and condemned criminals.

In 67 BCE, Pompey the Great of Rome invaded Pontus, and Mithridates (sometimes spelled Mithradates) retreated to the Black Sea. But Mithridates was familiar with the writings of Xenophon from four centuries before (see Oh, Honey, Don't!, p. 25). He lured the Roman army toward Trabzon, where he had left some pots of poisoned honey. A few squadrons of Roman soldiers feasted on the poisonous honey, fell ill, and were massacred by Mithridates's army.

Eventually, though, the Romans gained the upper hand, and Mithridates realized his enemies were close at hand. Ever the family man, he hastily gathered together all his wives, concubines, and younger children and poisoned them, sparing them the embarrassment of being paraded in chains through Roman streets. But when he tried to commit suicide by poison, it didn't work. The daily doses of poison he'd been taking for so long actually *had* given his body immunity.

Mithridates's final take-out order.

According to some accounts, he made one of his men slay him with the king's own sword.

The Romans found the recipe for Mithridates's antidote for poisoning, which contained as many as sixty-five ingredients. It became a popular antipoison drug for centuries after his death. Paranoid people in positions of power took daily doses of "mithridate" in an effort to protect themselves from poison.

ANCIENT ROMAN HAIR AND MAKEUP—GET THE LOOK!

Beehive plus unibrow— SO last millennium!

When in ancient Rome, do as the Romans did!

For makeup tips, we'll turn to those authorities of awesome—ancient Roman historians Ovid and Pliny the Elder—and their beauty dos and don'ts. Want to brighten a pasty face? DO try *cerussa* (a lead-based cosmetic), recommends Ovid. For additional brilliance, he suggests adding crocodile dung. Cheeks can be reddened with cinnabar (a red form of mercury) and *minium* (red lead), or, for more exotic ingredients, the contents of a crocodile's intestines. For even more effective blush, DO try mixing *minium* with bird poop, Pliny urges. Want to bring out your eyes? DO line them with *stibium* (an antimony-based substance).

DON'T pluck your eyebrows, agree our sources. Both applaud a unibrow as an ideal look. If your eyebrows don't naturally grow across the bridge of your nose, Ovid recommends using *stibium* to darken up the line.

DROP-DEAD GORGEOUS

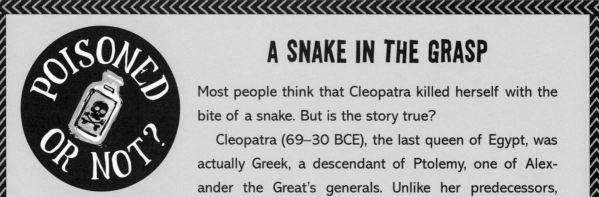

A SNAKE IN THE GRASP

Most people think that Cleopatra killed herself with the bite of a snake. But is the story true?

Cleopatra (69–30 BCE), the last queen of Egypt, was actually Greek, a descendant of Ptolemy, one of Alexander the Great's generals. Unlike her predecessors, though, she made the effort to learn Egyptian and was probably well regarded by her Egyptian subjects. Her foreign policy goal was to keep Egypt from being swallowed up by the powerful Roman Empire, but sadly for her, that plan failed. She anticipated that she might need to use poison for a dignified exit from the world in case the Romans conquered Egypt (which they eventually did). She preferred death to being captured and paraded through the streets of Rome. So she tested a variety of poisons on condemned prisoners and monitored the effects.

According to Shakespeare's play *Antony and Cleopatra*, Cleopatra ended her own life by holding an asp (a sort of venomous snake) up to her chest and enticing it to bite her. But Shakespeare was probably departing from the facts in order to create a more dramatic scene. It's unlikely that the asp story is true. Some historians believe she jabbed herself with a poisoned hairpin. Others think her Roman captors may have been responsible for her death.

Cleopatra's death was probably not this pretty.

I CAME, I SAW, I POISONED

The Roman Empire flourished for almost five centuries, from 27 BCE to 476 CE. Rome itself was a rich, powerful, sophisticated city, with huge public buildings, roads, aqueducts, and sewers. But the city was also drenched in poison.

There was the unintentional kind, most notably lead. Lead was a regular part of daily life—water pipes, storage urns, vessels, and paints were made with it, and Romans added it to wine to sweeten it. The lead acetate sweetener was known as *sapa*. Many upper-class Romans suffered from gout—a disease that results from the formation of sharp crystals of uric acid in the joints—and yes, that's as painful as it sounds. We now know that there's a direct association between gout and lead poisoning (see Nice Work: Painter, p. 60). Some historians believe the high level of exposure to lead may have contributed to the overall decline of Roman society. Lead builds up over time in your body and muddles your thinking. The Romans knew lead was dangerous, but the effects of lead poisoning were probably just one more ailment among many, and the longer-term, general ill health people suffered would have been difficult to trace directly to lead exposure.

But there was also a whole lot of the intentional kind: poison that was used for sinister purposes. The Romans knew about many plant-based poisons, including belladonna, aconite, hemlock, and opium. One Roman writer called aconite "mother-in-law's poison." Not-so-secret schools for learning to be a professional poisoner sprang up, as did a thriving market for antidotes, although most of them probably didn't work. It became fashionable for every rich and powerful person to employ a *praegustator,* or a food taster (see Nice Work: Food Taster, p. 16).

WITH FRIENDS LIKE THESE, WHO NEEDS ENEMAS?

An enema is a liquid medicine or "cleansing agent" that is introduced into your body through your, er, back end. In the past, enemas were also called clysters. Throughout history, poisoned enemas were a popular way to eliminate an enemy.

Bottoms up.

FAMILY FEUDS

One of ancient Rome's most notorious poisoners was Agrippina the Younger, most famous for being the mother of Nero.

She gave birth to Nero in 37 CE, and soon after, her husband died. Abruptly. Getting Nero onto the throne, says Roman writer Tacitus, became the ruling passion of his mother's life. At thirty-two she married her uncle, who was fifty-seven and who also happened to be the emperor. His name was Claudius. Agrippina persuaded Uncle Claudius/her new husband to adopt Nero, now in his teens, which he did.

Claudius already had a son, Britannicus, heir to the throne. (Still following this? Welcome to royal families.)

Soon enough, everyone who stood in Nero's path to becoming emperor began dropping dead. Food tasters must have been working triple-overtime.

Next to go was Claudius, who ate a dish of poisoned mushrooms and died after twelve hours of agony. (The writer Suetonius claimed that Claudius survived by vomiting up the mushrooms but was finished off by a poisoned enema.) At age sixteen, Nero became joint ruler with his younger stepbrother Britannicus (41–55 CE).

Agrippina—not exactly the Mother of the Era.

HEIR TODAY, GONE TOMORROW

A few months into their reign, Nero showed that he had learned at his mother's knee. He summoned the well-known poisoner Locusta and ordered her to prepare a poison for Britannicus. The first attempt failed. Says writer Tacitus, the boy received a dose of poison but "passed it off his bowels." Nero threatened Locusta with execution if the next effort didn't work. She assured him the next poison would work as quickly as a dagger.

Soon thereafter, at the banquet table, Britannicus's food taster sampled a cup of his master's soup and declared that it was too hot. Britannicus called for some cold water to cool it down. The cold water poured into the soup was laced with poison, and Britannicus fell to the floor, unable to talk or breathe and foaming at the mouth. Nero, it was reported, went on calmly eating while his stepbrother died.

Nero soon chafed at his mother's helicopter parenting. He didn't appreciate that she saw herself as a co-ruler and the imperial mother, so he had her sent away, but not far enough. He tried to poison her three times, but it didn't work. It seems she'd long feared being poisoned and knew how to protect herself with antidotes. So Nero had her lured onto a collapsible boat, designed to fall apart at sea. She swam to safety.

Then he arranged for a lead ceiling over her bed to fall on her. That malfunctioned.

Finally, in exasperation, Nero went to plan D and had his mother bludgeoned and stabbed to death, in 59 CE.

ROMAN EMPEROR

Being an emperor in Rome could be hazardous to your health. One of the many unpleasant side effects of lead poisoning is sterility (an inability to have children). Many emperors left no heirs—possibly because of lead poisoning—which may explain why so many emperors were bumped off by ambitious poisoners eager to gain the throne.

Emperors who probably died from intentional poisoning include Augustus, Claudius, Vitellius, Domitian, Hadrian, Commodus, Caracalla, and Alexander Severus. Many of them were so cruel that few people mourned their deaths.

According to the ancient Roman writer Cassius Dio, the empress Livia (58 BCE–29 CE) managed to poison her husband, Emperor Augustus, in spite of his paranoia about being poisoned. She smeared poison on figs still growing on a tree and invited him to pick the fruit himself. He fell ill and died.

Emperor Claudius—one of many in a long line of rulers who met a bitter enema.

4

POISONS, POTIONS, AND WITCHES' BREWS

The Middle Ages

So long as the mother, Ignorance, lives, it is not safe for Science,
the offspring, to divulge the hidden causes of things.
—Johannes Kepler

MALADIES AND MAGICK CURES

The people who lived during the Middle Ages did not think of themselves as living in the "middle" of anything. Like all people, they would have thought of themselves as living in modern times. Later historians came up with that phrase because they needed something to call the era of European history that occurred between the fall of the Roman Empire and the start of the Renaissance. The Middle Ages have also been called the Dark Ages, be-

Family dinner—medieval style.

cause they were times of constant warfare, feudalism, and poor personal hygiene. That's a pretty accurate description of what was going on in Europe from about 500 to 1400. But in other areas of the world, things didn't seem quite so dark. Grand civilizations continued to flourish. And wherever there were paths to power, people kept on poisoning one another.

THE MEAN QUEEN

Wu Zetian (624–705) was the only woman to rule China in more than three thousand years of its history. Being the one and only empress in a man's world could be a tough job.

She was a fan of poison as a way of removing difficult or inconvenient people in her path, although she didn't shy away from torture and creatively gruesome styles of execution when she felt inclined. Before she became empress, she may have poisoned her own mother and then had the wife of Emperor Gaozong murdered. After that she married Gaozong herself. She gave birth to four sons and a daughter. When the weak-willed emperor had a stroke, she took charge of governing. And then he died abruptly. Had she poisoned him?

Empress Wu.

In 683, she became the "dowager empress" (a widowed woman who is allowed to rule) for a succession of her sons. She continued to dispose of anyone who challenged her power, including, perhaps, her eldest son, who died suddenly—of poison?—at age twenty-four. She crushed a plot intended to overthrow her and dispensed with

nearly all members of her husband's imperial family. In 690 she ordered the last of her sons to abdicate (step down) and took power until shortly before her death, from natural causes, in 705.

All these events, whether or not they're true, contribute to Empress Wu's controversial reputation. But she stabilized the Tang dynasty at a time when it was at risk of crumbling. Also, much of her story was recorded for posterity by angry in-laws. And people who write history—until recently, nearly always men—haven't been very tolerant of strong female rulers.

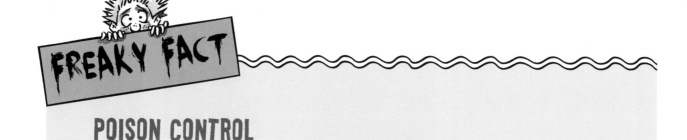

FREAKY FACT

POISON CONTROL

Chinese rulers during the Ching dynasty, which began in 1644, used silver chopsticks, which were thought to be able to detect the presence of poison—they were supposed to change color if there was poison in the food. Celadon dishes, and spoons made from the beak of a large bird, were said to have the same effect.

FUTILE FEUDALISM

Now let's turn to the heartland of western Europe, where most people were illiterate and deeply superstitious. Peasants toiled in the fields owned by their boss, usually a local lord, in exchange for his protection, should the town be attacked by neighboring dukedoms or vicious Vikings. The lord, in turn, reported to *his* boss, usually the king. It was a world dominated by absolute rulers and by the Church. Everyone believed that life and death were predetermined—if you were born a serf, you were meant to be poor. If you were born a duke, you were destined to have power and privilege. There wasn't much room for upward mobility. So there was little reason to remove people who blocked your way up the social ladder, because for most people, there *was* no ladder. But not for all people. Poison could make things possible if you happened to be, say, an ambitious cardinal or a second-born heir.

But the lack of social mobility didn't mean poison wasn't popular at all social levels. Ordinary people turned to poisons for different purposes. They believed in curses and hexes and love potions and magical cures, and they kept poison-potion makers in business. And, judging from the relatively large number of texts from this time that include directions for preparing antidotes, we can conclude that poisonings occurred frequently. Either that, or people were seriously paranoid.

A PAINLESS SMILE—GET THE LOOK!

He probably didn't floss regularly.

Want to keep your teeth in your mouth, however many you may have left? Here's a dental-care tip from the *Regimen Sanitatis Salernitanum,* written sometime during the twelfth or thirteenth century: "Gather the seeds of the leeks, / Burn them with the juice of the henbane, / And direct the smoke toward your teeth through a funnel."

Got a toothache? John of Gaddesden recommends poking the sore part with a needle that's been slimed with the guts of "a many footed worm which rolls up in a ball when you touch it." Problem solved!

DROP-DEAD GORGEOUS

MEDIEVAL MEDICINE

In the fifteen hundred years since ancient Greece, Western medicine didn't progress very far. Medieval physicians still considered the writings of the ancient Greek physicians, Galen and Hippocrates, to be the last word in medical knowledge. Hippocrates had declared that the elements—earth, air, fire, and water—controlled the body in the form of four liquids called the humors. To be healthy, one's humors had to be in balance. This made perfect sense to the medieval mind.

Magic and astrology were also a big part of medieval medical thinking. A ninth-century medical text describes a disease called Elfsickness, thought to be caused by tiny elves shooting tiny arrows into you. Physicians believed that knowing the position of the planetary bodies and how to balance the four humors were the pathways toward good health. If you were sick, it made sense to flush from your body whatever was out of balance. So most medical treatment involved making a patient barf, poop, sweat, or bleed. The barfing, pooping, and sweating were often brought about by giving the patient poisonous herbs or by a brisk rubdown with blister-beetle goop. The bleeding could involve an unclean knife and a basin, or a bowl of squirmy leeches. Use your imagination.

Taking medicines often caused . . . explosive results.

Another popular theory was known as *similia similibus curantur,* which means "treat like with like." Fans of this theory believed that everything God created had a use and that He left signs to show us how to use it all. Plants and animals that looked like body parts could be used to cure you. So bear grease was used to grow hair. Snake oil was used to limber up muscles. Walnuts, which kind of look like brains, were medieval smart-food. And, along the same line of thinking, the more dreadful the disease you had, the more powerful the medicine you ought to take. The line between a medicine and a poison was blurry. Local apothecary shops (medieval drugstores) stocked many dangerous poisons.

THE MIDDLE EAST IN THE MIDDLE AGES

Farther to the east, Arabs were living in the golden age of Islam, a religion founded by Muhammad (570–632). After Muhammad's death, the Islamic Empire spread from the Middle East and Persia, across modern-day Turkey, to North Africa, parts of Egypt, and, eventually, as far as Spain and southern France.

In the aftermath of the fall of the Roman Empire, as Vikings and other warrior tribes cut a murderous swath through Europe, looting treasures and destroying libraries, Arab scholars took custody of and safeguarded many of the ancient Greek and Roman texts about medicine, alchemy, and other classical scientific knowledge.

Arab scientists excelled in chemistry, and Arab scholars wrote many important books about medicinal plants and poisons and antidotes. In the eighth century, an Arab chemist successfully made arsenic trioxide, a tasteless, odorless powder that would be used as a go-to poison for murderers for the next thousand years.

An Arab doctor known in the West as Haly Abbas, who died in 994, introduced strychnine to the West (see Tox Box, p. 86) in his medical textbook, which described mysterious "nuts" with powerful medicinal properties. Strychnine has been used for

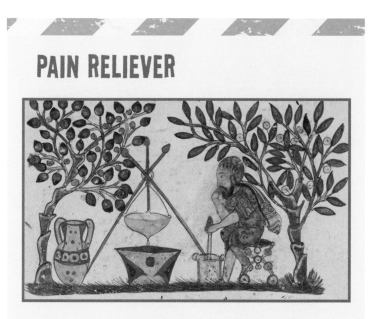

PAIN RELIEVER

Surgery was an ordeal in medieval Europe, after opiates and other painkillers fell out of favor with physicians. But physicians in the Islamic world developed many analgesics (pain relievers) from plants like henbane, hemlock, opium, and mandrake root.

both good and bad purposes since ancient times. It was probably known to the Malays and the Chinese by about 776 BCE.

Another famous Muslim scientist was Ibn Sina (980–1037), known in the Western world as Avicenna. He wrote a huge book about medicine. It described hundreds of plants that could be used as a source of drugs, including opium, which he recommended for treating various ailments. He also classified poisons as animal, vegetable, or mineral. Gradually, some of the Eastern medical knowledge made its way to Europe. Ibn Sina's medical textbook was translated into Latin and used in European universities for six centuries.

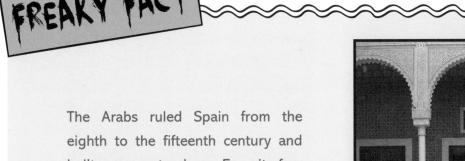

The Arabs ruled Spain from the eighth to the fifteenth century and built many vast palaces. Favorite features of luxurious Islamic courtyards were ornamental pools of mercury. Guests could dabble their fingers in the liquid metal—a beautiful but poisonous pastime.

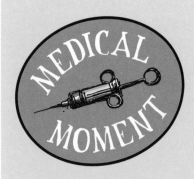

JUST PASSING THROUGH

In the Middle Ages, antimony (see Tox Box, p. 43) was a common go-to treatment for hangovers (sick feelings from drinking too much alcohol) and constipation (difficulty pooping). Wine was left overnight in a special goblet made of antimony. The person who was hungover or constipated drank it down the following morning, after the wine had absorbed some of the metal from the cup.

If you didn't have an antimony cup, you might have a perpetual pill on hand. Perpetual pills were small pellets of antimony. When swallowed, the poisonous metal pellet would irritate the stomach and "unclog" a person's intestines. The pill never dissolved or broke down, so it could be retrieved later, after the patient pooped it out. The pills could be reused after (one hopes) they'd been washed off. Does that sound better than a clyster? Tough call.

Wine infused with antimony—
the ultimate hangover remedy.

DEEP-ROOTED FEARS

The plant known as mandrake—featured in the Harry Potter series—contains a poison closely related to atropine (see Tox Box, p. 54). In medieval times, people thought that pulling out the mandrake plant by its roots caused it to scream and give off a foul

smell. They also thought that hearing it scream or smelling its odor would drive a person mad, so dogs were used to drag the roots from the ground. The roots were used as a poison, a treatment for asthma and epilepsy, a painkiller in surgery, and an aphrodisiac (love potion).

Pulling up a mandrake root is thirsty work for man's best friend.

Name: Antimony [AN-tih-moh-nee]

Other names: tartar emetic or stibnite (black antimony sulfide)

Source: Antimony is an element with the symbol Sb (from the Latin word *stibium*). Antimony is a brittle metal found naturally in the earth's crust, in stibnite and similar ores.

How it's delivered: Swallowed or breathed in

Effects: Severe sweating, stomach cramps, dehydration, vomiting, convulsions, coma, and possibly death. Smaller doses act as a laxative (they give you diarrhea).

SCRIBE

By the thirteenth century, the Christians had driven most of the Muslims out of Moorish Spain and southern France. Many of the Greek and Roman texts that had been preserved by Arab scholars were moved to monasteries in northern France, Germany, and Britain.

In monasteries, monks laboriously copied these books by hand in special rooms devoted to the purpose, called *scriptoria*. This was a time before the printing press had been invented (which happened in 1453). Books were rare

and extremely costly, not only because of the labor involved in hand writing and lavishly illustrating them, but also because paper was not yet available. The monks used expensive parchment made from the hides of calves, sheep, or goats.

Scribes worked long hours in unheated rooms, wearing scratchy, bug-infested robes, performing tedious, eye-straining work by candlelight or whatever light filtered in through the small (open) windows. To add to the dismal conditions, they worked with poisons to make their inks and paints. Tests of bones of medieval monk scribes show that many were poisoned by mercury. Mercury-based cinnabar was used to make a bright red ink.

5

THE WRETCHED RENAISSANCE

Or have we eaten on the insane root
That takes the reason prisoner?
—Shakespeare, *Macbeth*

STIRRING UP TROUBLE

The word "renaissance" means "rebirth." During the European Renaissance (which occurred from about 1400 to 1630), the fields of art, architecture, and science flourished. It was a time of religious turmoil, expanding trade, and global exploration. Some would also call it the golden age of poisoning.

A Renaissance sword—don't leave home without it.

It was a violent age—most gentlemen wouldn't dream of leaving home without their swords, much the way people feel about leaving home without their phones today. But killing a rival by poison was considered dishonorable and cowardly—the very opposite of a "fair fight." Poisoning was also widely feared by those in positions of power. A sixteenth-century lawyer called poison "the most horrible and fearfull to the nature of man, and of all others can be least prevented, either by manhood or by providence." Poisoners who were caught were executed hideously (see In the Soup, p. 49).

Still, a lot of poisoners weren't caught. Poisoning was difficult to prove in court. Neither scientists—known at the time as natural philosophers—nor physicians had the technology or know-how to detect poison in a body.

And even if a death looked suspicious, there were certain suspected poisoners that no one dared accuse because they were in positions of extreme power. Many kings, queens, and popes had poisoners on their payrolls. On that note, we will begin with just such a powerful family—the Borgias.

ALL IN THE FAMILY

The Borgias have been considered among the most notorious poisoners in history. Are the accusations justified?

The Borgias' rise to power began when Rodrigo Borgia (1431–1503) was elected pope, in 1492. He became Pope Alexander VI.

At the time, Italy wasn't yet a country—it was a bunch of smaller kingdoms that were often invaded by the more powerful France and Spain. Local rulers made their own laws and rounded up their own armies. They formed alliances with whoever served their own interests. And the local rulers were wary of the new pope. Before Rodrigo Borgia's election, practically all popes had been Italian, and Rodrigo was from Spain.

Rodrigo Borgia, who became Pope Alexander VI.

The new pope quickly placed members of his family in positions of power.

Although this was standard practice among popes of the day, the pope's favoritism did not go over well with many church higher-ups.

Rodrigo the Pope may have fathered two surviving Borgia offspring, Cesare (1476–1507) and

Lucrezia Borgia and her brother Cesare.

Lucrezia (1480–1519) while he was pope—a big no-no, since popes have never been allowed to have romantic relationships. Or they may have been his niece and nephew, as the pope claimed they were. Still, Rodrigo doted on Cesare and Lucrezia like a father. He elevated Cesare to the status of a prince. He met with many rich and powerful men vying to marry the beautiful Lucrezia. And Cesare didn't hesitate to get rid of his enemies, poison being one of his favorite weapons. Rumors flew that the pope and his "nephew" Cesare poisoned wealthy cardinals and noblemen so that they could take over their estates and enrich the church—and themselves.

Beautiful, fun loving, and well educated, Lucrezia had several broken engagements and three actual husbands. Some of these soul mates died mysteriously, while others realized it was better for their health to leave town so that her powerful father and brother could marry her off to someone more politically convenient. She was probably innocent of most of the accusations people leveled at her. Party girl she may have been, but likely not a poisoner. (She died at thirty-nine, ten days after the birth of a stillborn child, probably of complications from childbirth.)

DEAD RINGER

A favorite murder weapon of the Borgias, it was whispered, was a secret poison called *la cantarella,* which may have included some combination of arsenic, phosphorus, (see Tox Box, p. 93) lead acetate, and cantharidin (see Tox Box, p. 48). Or it might have been plain old, run-of-the-mill arsenic trioxide. Rumors circulated that the Borgias

opened a spring-loaded hatch on a hollow ring and poured the powder into enemies' drinks. Others talked of poisoned prongs on the underside of Cesare's ring, which could fatally prick his enemies with a handshake.

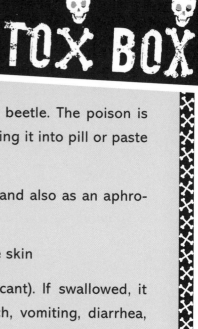

A ring with a hinge, which *might* have contained poison.

After a hot August night in 1503, having dined with a wealthy cardinal, both Cesare and Rodrigo woke up ill. It was rumored that they'd poisoned themselves by drinking wine intended for the cardinal, which had gotten mixed up in the kitchen. But it seems much more likely that both contracted malaria. (August in Rome was high season for malaria, which is transmitted by mosquitoes.) The pope lingered for thirteen days and then died. Cesare recovered but was pursued and killed by his enemies while still in a weakened state. We may never know just how many people were poisoned by this pope—and what was the true cause of the Borgias' deaths.

TOX BOX

Name: Cantharidin [kan-THAR-ih-din]

Other names: Also called cantharides or Spanish fly

Source: It's a chemical produced by certain species of beetle. The poison is made by grinding the dried insects into powder and mixing it into pill or paste form.

Popular poisonous products: Used as a wart remover and also as an aphrodisiac (a love potion).

How it's delivered: Swallowed or absorbed through the skin

Effects: Cantharidin is a blistering agent (called a vesicant). If swallowed, it causes burning pain in the mouth, throat, and stomach, vomiting, diarrhea, bleeding, coma, and death. If applied to the skin, it can raise painful blisters.

IN THE SOUP

In England in 1531, a man named Richard Roose slipped a deadly dose of poison (possibly hemlock and nightshade) into the soup—also called porridge—that was being prepared for a banquet given by John Fisher, the bishop of Rochester. Roose may have been the cook, or he may have been a friend of the cook's. Some accounts say he was bribed to do the job by enemies of the bishop.

The bishop himself declined to have soup that evening, but the poisoned soup made seventeen members of his household seriously ill. In those days, poor people often waited at the gates of large estates hoping for leftovers from feasts. Many of these people were also poisoned by the leftover porridge. Two people "died sodainly": a gentleman of the house named Bennet Curwen, and a poor widow named Alyce Tryppytt, and the rest "never recovered their healths till their dying day." As punishment, Roose was boiled alive.

FREAKY FACT

A popular poison throughout sixteenth-century Europe was made by feeding arsenic to toads and then distilling out the secretions from the dead toad. The poison was known as *venin de crapaud*.

MURKY MEDICINE

Medicine in the Renaissance was still mired in the Middle Age mind-set. Except for a couple of noteworthy exceptions (see The Doctor Was Dubious, p. 59, and Dr. Know-It-All, pp. 51–52), most medical practitioners continued to do more harm than good. Only the wealthy could afford physicians, who wore long robes and rarely touched their patients. A physician's main method of diagnosing patients was to take their pulse or to study their urine in a glass vial, judging its color, smell, and cloudiness.

Partly cloudy?

Sometimes the physician even tasted it. No wonder they overcharged patients.

Physicians also had an extremely sketchy knowledge of how the body is actually put together, because the church forbade cutting into bodies, and studying anatomy was considered unholy and forbidden. Christians were not allowed to dissect dead bodies for study until late in the fifteenth century. Yet physicians' lack of expertise in diagnosing a patient's condition didn't stop them from prescribing some toxic treatments.

If you needed more hands-on help, you visited a barber surgeon (see Barbaric Barber Surgeons, p. 51), who was much less expensive than a physician.

BARBARIC BARBER SURGEONS

Even if you could afford a physician (and most people couldn't), physicians were hard to come by—in 1568, there were only nine of them in London for a population of about 120,000 people. Commanding much less respect, but more freely available, were the barber surgeons. They could pull your tooth, give you a haircut, or give you an enema. Some could also perform simple surgeries, amputate limbs, and provide bleeding and cupping services (see Medieval Medicine, pp. 38–39). Cupping involved heating a special cup made of metal, glass, or ce-

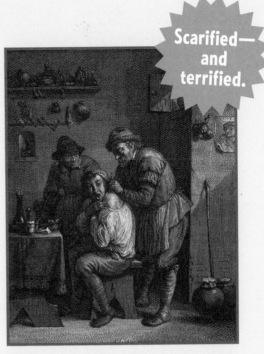

Scarified—and terrified.

ramic over the fire and then plopping it onto the patient's skin. It produced suction and raised a huge welt. For added excitement, you could be "scarified" first, which meant that cuts were made in the skin before the cup was applied. That was known, disturbingly, as wet cupping. Both methods were supposed to draw the "bad humors" from the body.

DR. KNOW-IT-ALL

Physician, botanist, and alchemist Philippus Aureolus Theophrastus Bombastus von Hohenheim bludgeoned his way onto the medical scene with bad manners and little respect for his physician colleagues. He rejected the teachings of Galen and Hippocrates and declared that the cause of disease might be due to other factors besides having unbalanced humors.

Paracelsus—a superior bragger.

He was born near Zurich, Switzerland, in 1493, and eventually took the name Paracelsus, a variation on the name of the ancient Roman physician Celsus, who lived in the first century CE. The name Paracelsus means "superior to Celsus." That pretty well sums up this guy's personality. Quarrelsome and cocky, he emphasized experimentation and chemical medications in addition to magical potions and astrology. He is generally considered the founder of the field of toxicology.

Paracelsus embraced the principle of "treat like with like" (see Medieval Medicine, pp. 38–39) and prescribed treatments for his patients that included mineral baths, mercury, lead, and arsenic. He studied silicosis (a disease commonly suffered by miners) and concluded that it was caused by the inhalation of poisonous vapors in the mines and was not, as people believed, revenge by mountain spirits. He introduced laudanum to the world—mostly a mixture of opium and alcohol, although, with his characteristic flair, Paracelsus added some crushed pearls, henbane, and frog spawn. Laudanum would be sold over the counter for the next several centuries, minus the frog spawn.

Modern toxicologists often quote Paracelsus's statement that "the dose makes the poison." He died in a tavern brawl at age forty-eight.

  **POISON**

THAT PALE RENAISSANCE COMPLEXION—GET THE LOOK!

Queen Elizabeth I of England wore thick lead makeup to hide her smallpox scars.

Want deathly white skin? Slather yourself from hairline to bustline with ceruse, which is made from lead. Problem with skin blemishes? Ceruse will cover up even the deepest scars from smallpox—you can spackle on as much as a half-inch layer! Top that off with egg white for a smooth sheen. Careful not to smile! Your makeup may crack. And be glad electric lighting hasn't been invented yet; in dim candlelight, no one will notice how your makeup turns a rather ghastly gray after a few hours.

Want to flirt from behind your fan? You can achieve that doe-eyed look with belladonna, an extract of the deadly nightshade plant (see Atropine Tox Box, p. 54). Add it to your eyes in drop form to dilate your pupils. Careful! It stings a lot!

DROP-DEAD GORGEOUS

An advice book from the late fifteenth century suggests this remedy for removing unwanted hair:

"Take 2 ounces of quicklime, 1 ounce of arsenic, and as much rock alum as you could fit in a chestnut, and grind it all together in a powder very well, then knead with gold. . . . Paste it where you want the hairs to fall out. Leave it for the time it takes to say two Our Fathers, then wash it off."

Name: Atropine [AT-ruh-peen]

Source: Atropine and its related poisons are found in certain plants, including deadly nightshade (*Atropa belladonna*), mandrake (*Mandragora*), black henbane (*Hyoscyamus niger*), and the plant *Datura stramonium,* which is known by many common names, including thorn apple, jimsonweed, and stinkweed. The leaves and roots can be dried and ground into a powder.

How it's delivered: Swallowed or absorbed through the skin

Effects: Dilated pupils, blurred vision, trembling, dizziness, intense thirst, double vision, nausea, hallucinations, delirium, aggressive behavior, rambling speech, rapid heartbeat, and unconsciousness. With a toxic dose, the poison paralyzes the nervous system and death may occur within half an hour after swallowing.

A GLOVE STORY

Catherine de Medici (1519–1589) was the Italian-born wife of the French king, Henry II. If some accounts are to be believed, Catherine poisoned her way to becoming queen of France. Did the young Catherine, as has been alleged, poison her new husband Henry's older brother, François, heir to the throne, so that her husband could be first in line for king? After playing tennis on a hot day and downing a glass of water, Francois collapsed suddenly and died a short time later. He probably died of pleurisy (inflamed lungs), but the faithful servant who'd given him the water was accused of being in cahoots with Catherine. He was torn apart by horses as punishment.

Despite their unhappy marriage, Catherine and Henry II had ten children. Three of Catherine's sons would grow up to become French

Catherine de Medici.

kings. But the French mistrusted their Italian-born queen, and accusations of poisoning continued to be whispered. Did she kill her son's future mother-in-law, Jeanne de Navarre, by sending her a pair of poisoned gloves two months before the wedding? Could it be possible that she even poisoned her three sons, King Francis II, Charles IX, and Henry III, as was rumored?

All extremely unlikely. Strong female rulers have always been viewed with suspicion (see The Mean Queen, pp. 35–36).

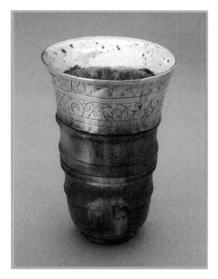

Ye olde poison detector—this cup made of silver and rhinoceros horn supposedly changed color if the drink contained poison.

But no one would suggest that she was *nice*. A Catholic, she detested Huguenots (French Protestants), and she almost certainly played a role in inciting the notorious massacre of Huguenots on St. Bartholomew's Day in 1572, and in the subsequent Wars of Religion. And she certainly had poisoners in her employ. The French credited Catherine with introducing Italian poisoning methods to France. Henry of Navarre, who would eventually succeed Catherine's son Henry III and become Henry IV, was rumored to have been so worried about being poisoned when visiting the French court that he ate only eggs he had cooked himself and drank only water he had personally scooped from the river.

BEARS AND GOATS AND ANTIDOTES

France wasn't the only country with poison problems. Across the English Channel, members of the English court of Elizabeth I (1533–1603) were keeling over with equally alarming frequency.

With Elizabeth's court awash in poison, the market for antidotes skyrocketed. Fossilized sea animals were popular. Known as St. Cuthbert's beads or fairy money, they were strung on necklaces or set into rings and supposedly grew hot in the presence of poison. Bezoars were also big. (A bezoar is a hard object found in the digestive tracts of goats and other animals.) They were considered a surefire way to neutralize any poison. People wore them on chains and dunked them into their food. Powdered mummy added to your food

Bezoars— decorative jewelry and disgusting antidotes!

Many people were hornswoggled into thinking they were buying real unicorn horns.

was also thought to work. If you were quite wealthy, you might invest in a precious gem for protection from poison. Royalty drank from cups carved from a "unicorn" horn. It was widely believed that if your drink contained poison, the horn would cause it to bubble. As unicorns didn't actually exist, the unicorn horns were usually made from the long tusks of narwhals. Those who couldn't afford an entire horn could buy a smaller amount in powdered form, mix it with water or wine, and drink it. One physician writing in 1651 claimed, "It can scarce be said, whether to the Bezaar stone, or to the Unicornes horn the common people attributes greater vertues, for those are thought to be the prime Antidotes of all."

Dippy

In 1568, Queen Elizabeth arrested her cousin Mary, Queen of Scots. Mary had obvious ambitions to overthrow Elizabeth and take over the throne of England. During her long imprisonment, Mary was deeply concerned about being poisoned. She requested a unicorn's horn so that she could dip it in her food. It didn't do her much good in the long run, as in 1587 Elizabeth had her beheaded.

REST IN PIECES: DR. LOPEZ

The personal physician to Queen Elizabeth I, Rodrigo Lopus, or Lopez (1525–1594), was a Portuguese Jew who converted to Christianity. As with many Jews who had converted to Christianity during this intolerant time, people suspected that he might still be secretly practicing his old religion, and many distrusted him.

As the queen's doctor, Lopez grew prosperous and famous, but in 1593 he was accused of conspiring with the Spanish (at the time, enemies of England) to poison the queen. He maintained his innocence to the end, and the queen delayed signing his death warrant for many months. But in June of 1594 he was hanged, drawn, and quartered. He was probably innocent.

Three years after Lopez's execution, William Shakespeare wrote a play called *The Merchant of Venice.* The main character is a Jewish man named Shylock, quite possibly based on poor Dr. Lopez.

Dr. Lopez (right) conspires with a Spanish spy.

THE DOCTOR WAS DUBIOUS

A few years after Paracelsus died (see Dr. Know-It-All, pp. 51–52), another forward-thinking Renaissance doctor appeared on the scene: the French surgeon Ambroise Paré (ca. 1510–1590). When Paré began practicing medicine, surgery had a low sta-

tus among practitioners (see Barbaric Barber Surgeons, p. 51). Paré became a war surgeon for the French army. Thanks to the invention of the printing press and his ability to publish popular texts about his work, he gained fame and respect for his writings on battle-field surgery. He eventually became a surgeon to the stars, most notably to Catherine de Medici's sons, the three French kings.

Ambroise Paré.

Paré published a pamphlet that scorned expensive poison antidotes such as unicorn horns and powdered mummy. "Unicorne," he sniffed, "is not the proper name of any beast in the world, and that it is a thing onely feigned by Painters, and Writers of natural things, to delight the readers and beholders."

When Charles IX of France received an expensive bezoar stone as a gift, Paré assured the king that it would not be effective against poison. He even offered to prove his point on the spot. One of the king's cooks, sentenced to be hanged for theft, was summoned. Paré offered the condemned man a choice: he could opt to be hanged, or he could swallow a deadly poison along with the king's new bezoar stone and hope it would protect him. The condemned man chose the poison with the bezoar but died in agony. Charles, in turn, concluded the bezoar had been a fake.

PAINTER

The health hazards of working with paint have been known since medieval times. In his book *Il libro dell'arte,* Cennino Cennini cautioned painters against working with realgar, an arsenic-based red pigment. "There is no keeping company with it. . . . Look out for yourself."

Another early champion of workers' health issues was the Italian physician Bernardino Ramazzini. "Of the many painters I have known," he wrote, "almost all I found unhealthy."

In fact, many painters *were* made ill by their job. The common affliction known as painter's colic was characterized by paleness, tooth loss, fatigue, gout, and paralysis. Possible famous sufferers included Correggio, Raphael, Michelangelo, Francisco Goya, and Vincent van Gogh. Goya suffered from trembling hands, blindness, and dizziness. As recently as the twentieth century, an

In this fresco by Raphael, one figure appears to be his friend Michelangelo.
You can see that his knee is swollen, probably from paint- and wine-induced gout.

artist named Candido Portinari was diagnosed with lead poisoning and advised by his doctors to switch to less-toxic paints. He died in 1962, poisoned by his pigments.

A BRUSH WITH DEATH

In the paint boxes of most painters, from ancient Egyptian times onward, many paint pigments were poisonous. What were they made of?

RED: Made from cinnabar, which is the principal ore of mercury. Or you could heat together sulfur and mercury to form an artificial cinnabar. (Heating up mercury? Never a good plan.) Mercury sulfide made a red paint called vermilion.

BLUE: The beautiful Prussian blue contained cyanide and was a favorite of artists.

WHITE: Made from lead or antimony.

GREEN: Often made from arsenical compounds. The beautiful Scheele's green, named after Carl Scheele (see Nice Work: Scientist, pp. 124–125), and which was made from copper arsenite, was widely available by 1778. J. M. W. Turner was a fan of it. Manet painted with it in the 1860s.

YELLOW: Orpiment, also called king's yellow, was made from a volcanic stone with a sparkly quality that was found all over the world. It was extremely poisonous, as it, too, contained arsenic. Naples yellow, made from lead antimonate, was used as early as 500 BCE and probably colored the tiles of King Nebuchadnezzar's palace in Babylon.

CRIME AND CORRUPTION
The Sinister Seventeenth Century

In the most obscure, difficult and dangerous maladies it is better
to hazard a doubtful remedy than to give nothing at all.
—E. R. Arnaud

SUPER-SMELLY AND SUPERSTITIOUS

Good personal hygiene was not a top priority for Europeans living in the seventeenth century. Most people were unenthusiastic about bathing. They believed that soaking one's body in water opened up the pores to infection, disease, and even poison, according to the especially paranoid. Instead of bathing, the well-to-do doused their unwashed bodies with perfume and slathered their pocked faces with cosmetics. But perfumes and cosmetics often proved more dangerous than bathing, as many contained toxic ingredients. And it's anyone's guess how often deliberate poisonings occurred. Assassins may have slipped lethal doses of poison into bathing water, food, drinks, medicines, cosmetics, clothes, and perfumes.

Meanwhile, in the Western world, seventeenth-century physicians were not especially open to trying new tactics when it came to treating patients. Like most people, they believed that supernatural forces such as planetary bodies, evil omens, and witches could affect a person's health. And they continued to give their patients medicines that made them bleed, poop, barf, and, all too often, expire.

LIFE EXPECTANCY: A MATTER OF LIFE AND DEATH

Statistics on life expectancy can be tricky. In seventeenth-century England, for instance, the average life expectancy hovered around thirty-five. If you could survive childhood, you could expect to live to a ripe old age. Sadly, though, 12 percent of babies did not live to see their first birthday. Out of one hundred live births, sixty children would die before the age of sixteen. Those girls who survived to become mothers themselves faced serious peril during childbirth. Cities were death traps, due to epidemics and overcrowding. Unsurprisingly, wealthy people lived longer than laborers.

WHAT AILED THEM

Sudden deaths happened with dismaying frequency in the seventeenth century, and the causes were usually hard to determine. A quick scan of England's Bills of Mortality of the mid-1600s tells us that people died from "dog bytes," "lethargy," "grief," "fryght," "head mould," "stopping of the stomach," and "vomiting." Or we just get the perplexing adverb "suddenly." You see the problem.

The custom of recording how people died is an ancient one. The Romans kept death registries in their temples, and in medieval times, lists were compiled from at least the fourteenth century in many European countries. As early as 1538 in

England, Henry VIII ordered registries to be kept in every parish. The system was intended to give the well-to-do a heads-up to leave town in case of plague or some other epidemic.

In England these lists were compiled by local churches and were based on information gathered by the Searchers, who were workers employed by the parish. Their job was to go into homes and hospitals and inspect the newly departed and diagnose the cause of death. Searchers were usually old women, and it's doubtful that they had much medical training. It's also pretty unlikely that they could have recognized a death that had been caused by poison.

But the winds of change were stirring. With the 1600s came the first autopsies—the cutting up of dead people to determine what might have killed them. Important people were autopsied immediately, often in front of their grieving—and quickly grossed out—loved ones. Seventeenth-century microscopes weren't very powerful,

so investigators could not yet tell from the looks of a dead person's guts if that person had been poisoned. Still, when a death seemed truly suspicious, they fed some of the dead person's stomach contents to a dog to see if it got sick or died from whatever had been the deceased's last meal. Or they took a piece of the dead person's stomach, ground it up, mixed it into an ointment, and rubbed it onto a small animal such as a rabbit. If the animal's skin blistered, poison was most likely present.

Sometimes the person performing the autopsy might *taste* the dead person's bodily fluids to see if he could detect caustic substances.

The Diseases and Casualties this Week.

Disease	Count	Disease	Count
		Imposthume	1
		Infants	7
		Kingsevill	1
		Mouldfallen	1
		Kild accidentally with a Carbine, at St. Michael Wood-street	1
		Overlaid	1
Abortive	2	Rickets	9
Aged	32	Rising of the Lights	2
Bleeding	1	Rupture	2
Childbed	5	Scalded in a Brewers Mash, at St. Giles Cripplegate	1
Chrisoms	9		
Collick	1	Scurvy	4
Consumption	65	Spotted Feaver	2
Convulsion	41	Stilborn	13
Cough	5	Stopping of the Stomach	11
Dropsie	43	Suddenly	1
Drowned at S Kathar. Tower	1	Surfeit	7
Feaver	47	Teeth	27
Flox and Small-pox	15	Tissick	12
Flux	3	Ulcer	1
Found dead in the Street at Stepney	1	Vomiting	1
		Winde	1
Griping in the Guts	15	Wormes	1

Christned ⎰ Males — 121 ⎱
       ⎰ Females — 111 ⎱
       ⎰ In all — 232 ⎱

Buried ⎰ Males — 195 ⎱
    ⎰ Females — 198 ⎱ Plague
    ⎰ In all — 393 ⎱

Decreased in the Burials this Week —— 69

Parishes clear of the Plague —— 130   Parishes Infected —— 0

The Assize of Bread set forth by Order of the Lord Maier and Court of Aldermen,
A penny Wheaten Loaf to contain Eleven Ounces, and three
half-penny White Loaves the like weight.

HUSBANDS! GET THAT DEATHLY WHITE COMPLEXION.

WIVES! GET THAT VERY DEAD HUSBAND— TWO PRODUCTS IN ONE!

This being the seventeenth century, guys get to wear makeup, too—and lace and high heels and elaborate curls. Guys—if you're after that chalky-white look, try the new makeup called Aqua Toffana! Feeling ill? Uh-oh! Maybe you should have been nicer to your wife!

Dreadful detail: The poisonous makeup called Aqua Toffana was invented in 1625 by a woman named—you guessed it—Toffana, who was from Palermo, Sicily. Her product was chockablock with liquid arsenic. As many as six hundred men may have been poisoned by their wives. The exact method by which they were poisoned remains murky—wives may have tipped a few drops of the makeup into their husbands' wine over the course of days or weeks. Some accounts say they died quickly, in agony. Others say that the potion worked very slowly and that their demise took much longer.

Sometimes love is lethal.

At long last, someone noticed that a *lot* of well-to-do husbands seemed to have died and that there were just as many not-very-sad new widows around town. By this time, La Toffana had been operating her hush-hush operation for as many as fifty years. Inquiries were made, and a secret society was discovered in which wives received instructions on how to administer poisons. La Toffana was eventually captured and gruesomely executed. Many of the widows who had used her product fled or were banished, and a few were executed.

DROP-DEAD GORGEOUS

DISORDER IN THE COURT: POISON IN FRANCE

Over in France, poisoning had become an epidemic at the court of Louis XIV. Seventeenth-century Paris was teeming with shady apothecaries, alchemists, astrologers, and people who practiced the "dark arts."

A major scandal unfolded when the French chief of police began hearing rumors that lots of people were confessing to their priests that they'd poisoned someone. (In the Catholic Church, confession is the act of telling a priest about your sins and asking for forgiveness.) What made the situation even trickier was that a lot of these poisoners were members of the king's royal court. Word reached the king, and Louis established a committee to investigate the poisonings. The source of the poison was eventually traced back to a woman named Catherine Monvoisin, who became known as La Voisin. Not everything she sold was meant for murder, investigators discovered. Many had visited La Voisin for a love potion or a good-luck charm, or to have their fortune told. But she certainly did sell deadly poisons. Historians believe her murderous brew was some combination of arsenic, aconite, belladonna, and opium.

The committee uncovered the identities of many people who had been customers of La Voisin, and a good number were members of the noblest families of France. Even Jean Racine, a famous playwright, had been a customer of hers. His mistress had died suddenly and poisoning was suspected, but he was never arrested.

In 1679, 442 people were charged with murder. In 1680, La Voisin and thirty-five others—mostly "witches," fortune-tellers, and poison vendors—were executed. But

when the king's own mistress, Madame de Montespan, was found to have visited La Voisin, he finally called off the investigation. She swore she'd only been seeking a love potion to give to the king, but she still could have been arrested for treason. By the time the investigation ended, thirty-six people had been burned at the stake, four were condemned to row in the galleys of French royal navy ships, thirty-six were ruined financially by being banished from court or heavily fined, and eighty-one were chained up in prison for the rest of their lives.

Still, a lot of people had gotten away with murder.

SUDDEN DEATH				
☠	MINUTES	HOURS	DAYS	YEARS
ARSENIC			1-3	
LEAD				1-5
MERCURY		10-100		
ACONITE	3			
CYANIDE	0-5			

DEATH BY DOCTORS

King Charles II (1630–1685) ruled England during a tumultuous time in history. He was a first cousin of the French king, Louis XIV (see Disorder in the Court, p. 67), and, although secretly Catholic, he ruled as a Protestant king during those troubled times of religious unrest. Tall and handsome, Charles was liked by most of his subjects—they even named a dog breed after him (the King Charles spaniel). He was keenly interested in science and alchemy and had a lab built in his palace at Westminster.

He probably spent too much time in his alchemy lab, because some historians think the kidney failure he developed may have been the result of breathing in poisonous mercury vapors. The usually good-humored king began having bouts of irritation.

On a Sunday in 1685, the king felt suddenly unwell and had no appetite for his goose-egg omelet, usually his favorite meal. On Monday morning he staggered out of bed, cried out, and fainted. Fourteen of the best physicians in the land were hastily summoned to the bedside of the ailing king. Well-meaning but overzealous, they bled him, cupped him (see Barbaric Barber Surgeons, p. 51), shaved his scalp and rubbed it with blister-raising cantharidin (see Tox Box, p. 48), dosed him with antimony and mummy powder, slathered pigeon poop on his feet, stuck him with a red-hot poker, blew hellebore up his nostrils, administered several enemas, and bled him some more. Ever the considerate guy, the exhausted king apologized to his doctors for taking so long to die. By Friday, he was dead.

King Charles II.
(Not his real hair.)

Both the original King Charles spaniel and its more modern relation, the Cavalier King Charles spaniel (shown here), were named after King Charles II (left).

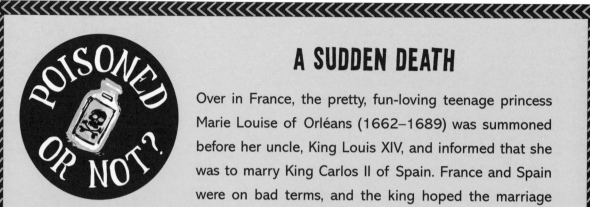

A SUDDEN DEATH

Over in France, the pretty, fun-loving teenage princess Marie Louise of Orléans (1662–1689) was summoned before her uncle, King Louis XIV, and informed that she was to marry King Carlos II of Spain. France and Spain were on bad terms, and the king hoped the marriage would smooth relations.

The princess was distraught. Carlos was the product of too much inbreeding among his Habsburg ancestors, who often married their close relatives to keep their bloodlines pure. He had inherited serious physical and mental deficiencies as a result. Marie Louise's husband-to-be was dim-witted, with an overly large head, a hard time chewing, and frequent epileptic-like fits. He also drooled a lot. The marriage took place anyway.

Carlos II . . .

. . . and his bummed-out bride, Marie Louise.

Marie Louise endured ten years at the dreary Spanish court, where she was hated for being French and for failing to produce an heir (although the fact that she had no children was a surprise to no one, given her husband's physical problems). Then, in 1689, at just twenty-seven, she died suddenly after two days of agony. It was rumored she'd been poisoned with arsenic. No one could tell for sure, because the field of forensic toxicology was three centuries away.

Ten years later, the king decided it would be fun to take a field trip. His choice of destination? The royal tombs. Once there, he demanded that the graves of some of his relations be opened, including that of his dead wife, Marie Louise. As her grave clothes were unfolded, witnesses reported that her face looked like that of someone who was merely sleeping. Her cheeks were still smooth and pink, her lips delicate. One of the characteristics of arsenic poisoning is that it preserves corpses long after death. Could the poison rumors be true?

FREAKY FACT

Arsenic breaks down very slowly in a dead body and can usually be found in a victim's hair, fingernails, and bones. It can be measured in the roots of a victim's hair as soon as half an hour after it's swallowed. Taxidermists (people who preserve dead animals for display) used to use arsenic because it interferes with decomposition.

YOU SAY POTATO, I SAY BE CAREFUL

Seventeenth-century Europeans believed that potatoes were poisonous. And, fun fact, they weren't entirely wrong: potatoes are members of the deadly nightshade family, and potato plants contain a poisonous chemical compound called solanine. It's a nerve toxin produced in the leaves, stem, and any green spots on the potato skin (which is why it's not a great idea to eat green potatoes).

Outside of Ireland, potatoes were used primarily as hog food. But after a series of crop failures and famines, the Prussian emperor Frederick the Great (1712–1786) commanded Prussian peasants to grow potatoes. He distributed free "seed potatoes" to all the farmers in his realm. Faced with their continued reluctance, the emperor announced that any farmer who didn't grow potatoes would have his nose and ears cut off. That seemed to work.

FREAKY FACT

At the court of Louis XIV, enemas were extremely fashionable—they were thought to be good for your complexion and to keep the mind sharp. The king had as many as four enemas a day—sometimes in full view of government officials and advisers. Certain pharmacists specialized in enemas and hung huge, plunger-shaped wooden plaques outside their shops.

CEREAL KILLER

Since medieval times, a mysterious disease had periodically roared through villages and struck down entire populations, terrifying Europeans. People called it St. Anthony's fire. Victims experienced unbearable burning sensations and blackening of the limbs. A related, also dreaded disease was called St. Vitus's dance. Victims experienced convulsions, hallucinations, feelings of suffocation, and weird, maniacal twitching that looked like a horrifying dance. People danced uncontrollably until they collapsed from exhaustion. Everyone believed they'd been cursed by witches and possessed by the devil.

Lots of hypotheses have been suggested as to the cause of these dance outbreaks,

Three boys afflicted with St. Vitus's dance. You wouldn't want to be invited to this dance.

including epilepsy, typhus, and some sort of mass hysteria. But one plausible explanation for the epidemics is that they were caused by the bread people were eating and a toxic fungus it contained, now known as ergot (see Tox Box, p. 74).

Poor people often ate two or three pounds of bread a day and not much else, so they were the most at risk. If you eat a lot of it, ergot causes a disease known as ergotism. The convulsive form can damage the nerves. The writhing, tremors, and delusions were called fits, and to superstitious people, the symptoms really did seem like the work of an evil enchantment. People reported sensations of being pricked with something sharp, or the feeling of bugs crawling all over their bodies. Others imagined seeing blood running down the walls.

Ergot was more likely to form on rye when the preceding winter was cold or

FREAKY FACT

An outbreak of St. Anthony's fire killed as many as forty thousand people in tenth-century France.

when there was a wet, cloudy spring, which length-
ened the time the flowers were open and made the
plant more vulnerable to infection. You could also
get the disease from eating moldy bread.

Ergotism tended to affect children and teenagers
more severely. People concluded that the afflicted
children had been bewitched and went looking for
witches. The targets of witch hunts tended to be the
"healers" in a village, usually older women with knowledge of the medicinal properties of herbs (see Nice Work: Wise Woman, p. 76).

Scientists have traced the location of witch trials in western Europe between 1580
and 1650 and have discovered that they were concentrated in places where rye was
the staple cereal and when the weather was both cold and wet and therefore ideal for
the production of ergot (see Poisoned or Not? The Witch Hunts, pp. 78–79).

Name: Ergot [UHR-gaht]

Source: Ergot is a plant mold that contains a group
of poisonous chemicals. It infests rye, wheat, barley,
and other grains, particularly during rainy seasons.

How it's delivered: Swallowed

Effects: There are two types of ergot poisoning. Gangrenous ergotism, also
known as holy fire or St. Anthony's fire, causes swelling and blackening in the
hands and feet. (Sometimes body parts actually fall off.) Convulsive ergotism, also known as St. Vitus's dance, produces feelings of numbness, intoxica-
tion, suffocation, seizures, vomiting, twitching, hallucinations, and a burning
sensation.

NEW WORLD DISORDER

When English settlers first landed at what became the colony of Jamestown, Virginia, in 1607, they found a familiar plant called *Datura stramonium,* a hardy weed that seemed to grow everywhere. (Other historians think they might have brought it along with them unintentionally.) It became known as jimsonweed, or Jamestown weed, a member of the nightshade family that contains a toxic chemical (see Atropine Tox Box, p. 54).

Nearly seventy years later, in 1676, some British soldiers arrived in Jamestown to restore order among the colonists in what has become known as Bacon's Rebellion. The soldiers gathered jimsonweed leaves "for a boil'd salad." Soon thereafter, the colonists watched as most of them "turned natural fools" for the next eleven days. One sat naked in a corner and acted like a monkey; another "would blow up a feather in the air"; another "would fondly kiss and paw his companions." By the time they recovered, the conflict had fizzled, when the leader of the uprising, Nathaniel Bacon, died suddenly, probably of dysentery.

WISE WOMAN

What did poor people do when they needed medical attention? Physicians were for the wealthy. Even the local apothecary was too expensive for the average person. Two options were available to most people: you could try prayer, or you could visit your local wise woman.

Most villages had a healer, or "wise woman," someone skilled in the use of medicinal plants—and she was often the only health practitioner available. Besides getting medical treatment, you could also ask her to remove a hex on your cow or whip up a love potion to woo the boy next door. She was as poor as everyone else and generally accepted payment in the form of food or home repairs. Her folk remedies were made of herbs and other plants that grew in the surrounding area. She often mixed these poisonous plants into disgusting concoctions. Some of these tried-and-true treatments were written down. Medieval medical books are full of "receipts" (recipes) that involve dead animal parts and dung. Leeches and snails were also popular ingredients. Sometimes these remedies contained ingredients that actually helped, or at least did less harm than the treatments wealthier people received from physicians. (People didn't call them doctors until the end of the seventeenth century.)

But this was a deeply superstitious time—everyone believed in trolls and bad spirits and, of course, witches. The better a wise woman was at her job, the more magical her cures seemed. It was a high-risk profession—when strange afflictions or unwanted behaviors cropped up, people's minds quickly jumped to supernatural explanations, and all too often they accused the wise woman of practicing black magic (see A Mother at Stake, p. 77).

A wise woman wearing an unwise fashion combination.

A MOTHER AT STAKE

Katharina Kepler (1546–1622) was a local healer living in what is now Germany. She sold herbal medicines, painkillers, and sleeping potions. She was also the mother of astronomer Johannes Kepler. This was a time when few women had the opportunity for higher education, and Katharina had never learned to read or write. But her son Johannes had shown great promise at school, and his education was supported by a wealthy nobleman.

Katharina wasn't well liked around the village. It was bad enough that her son was a scientist whose teachings had been condemned by the church, but she'd also had an aunt who had been burned at the stake for witchcraft. Sharp tongued and bad tempered, she didn't respond well when a woman in the village claimed that Katharina had tried to poison her. In 1616, she was accused of witchcraft and sentenced to death.

Her imprisonment and trial dragged on for several years, but after painstaking efforts, Johannes was able to prove that there was no real evidence against his mother. He secured her release and saved her from being burned at the stake.

Katharina Kepler and one of her interrogators, who is helpfully showing her his favorite torture instruments.

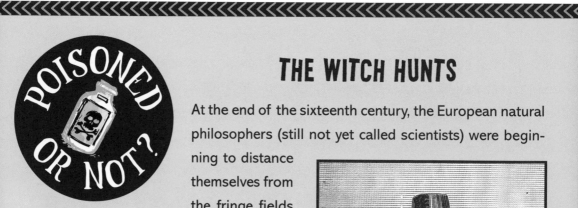

THE WITCH HUNTS

At the end of the sixteenth century, the European natural philosophers (still not yet called scientists) were beginning to distance themselves from the fringe fields of alchemy and astrology. But the forces of superstition continued to hold back scientific progress. People still believed in hexes, poxes, and black magic. Demonic possession was a disease you could diagnose in a patient, like epilepsy.

In Scotland, as many as eight thousand women were accused of being witches between 1560 and 1600 and were burned at the stake. In England, Queen Elizabeth I passed a law in 1562 that made witchcraft a crime punishable by death. For over a hundred more years, people continued to believe in witchcraft.

Which leads us to Salem, Massachusetts. In early 1692, a wave of strange behaviors struck some young residents of the town. Eight girls appeared to be possessed by the devil—they suffered "fits" and claimed to be experiencing a terrifying sensation of being pinched, pricked,

Matthew Hopkins was a notorious English witch-finder of the middle seventeenth century. His methods for forcing "witches" to confess bordered on torture.

and bitten by invisible forces. Similar strange afflictions were happening in several other nearby communities. Also, a bunch of cows dropped dead. What other explanation could there be for this behavior but a witch's curse? Neighbor accused neighbor, and hundreds of "witches" were rounded up. Nineteen people were executed for witchcraft.

Could ergotism have caused the girls' fits (see Cereal Killer, pp. 72–74)? Records indicate that the growing season in 1691 was unusually warm and wet, and it was likely to have caused the growth of the ergot mold in the stored grain. It's one of many theories that explain the girls' behavior, but a plausible one, to be sure.

An artist from the nineteenth century
imagining a scene from the Salem witch trials.

7

MURDER AND MEDICINE IN THE AGE OF REASON

God heals, and the doctor takes the fee.
—Ben Franklin

THE CHEMISTRY SET

By the eighteenth century, a new wave of thinking was emerging. The period would later come to be known as the Age of Reason. Scientists were discovering the natural laws of the universe, challenging ideas based only on faith, and advancing knowledge through the scientific method.

As the field of chemistry dawned, the new-found scientific knowledge was used for both good and bad purposes. Previously unknown poisons awaited the unsuspecting consumer in the forms of food, medicine, and a new product called tobacco.

A passionate fight over the best way to treat a patient. Medicine wasn't always reasonable in the Age of Reason.

NASTY HABIT FROM THE NEW WORLD

First, a little tobacco backstory. The tobacco plant originated in North America and had been known to the native people for thousands of years. Early on, it was probably smoked during sacred ceremonies by priests and medicine men, but the habit was gradually adopted by regular Maya and Aztecs.

When Columbus and his men sailed across the Atlantic and landed on an island in what is now the Bahamas, the native Arawaks offered the strangers gifts. Columbus wrote in his notebook that "the natives brought fruit, wooden spears, and certain dried leaves which gave off a distinct fragrance."

Unsure why anyone would want a bunch of dry leaves, Columbus and his men tossed them. Later that year, while exploring Cuba, two of Columbus's crew members, Rodrigo de Jerez and Luis de Torres, observed people smoking. Jerez took up the habit and returned to Spain. But the sight of him blowing smoke out his nose and mouth so alarmed people that he was put in prison by the Inquisition (a religious court that persecuted people who were thought to have anti-church beliefs). He was released several years later—and by then, more people had taken up smoking.

A Five-Alarm Habit

One of the first world travelers to popularize tobacco smoking in England was the explorer Sir Walter Raleigh (1552–1618). According to one story, a servant who saw him smoking was so alarmed, he doused his master with a bucket of water, believing Raleigh was on fire.

Blowing Smoke: Tobacco Gets Trendy

The Europeans didn't fully take to tobacco until around the mid-1500s. In 1560, Frenchman Jean Nicot introduced tobacco to France (nicotine is named after him). He presented a sample of tobacco to Catherine de Medici, queen of France (see A Glove Story, pp. 55–56). She preferred the dried leaves crushed into a powder so that they could be sniffed rather than smoked. The "snuff" habit became all the rage at the French court.

Smokerface

Tobacco contains a poisonous chemical called nicotine (see Tox Box, p. 83), and nicotine is addictive. So once Europeans started using tobacco, they wanted more and more, and demand grew. By the early 1600s, tobacco cultivation increased in the American colonies, and trade with Europe became extremely profitable. Tobacco was grown in the Chesapeake area, primarily in Virginia and Maryland, and American colonists shipped hundreds of thousands of pounds of it to England and Europe. People on both sides of the Atlantic took up the habit, which rapidly spread around the world.

One of the first links in a chain of misery caused by the tobacco plant—enslaved workers drying and preparing tobacco leaves.

By 1634, the English colonists in the West Indies, Bermuda, and Virginia were producing well over a million pounds of tobacco a year. And by 1650, it was ten million.

But growing tobacco was a lot of work. At first growers imported indentured servants from Europe, but by 1720, slaves from Africa became the primary source of labor on tobacco plantations. The demand for this addictive plant and the wealth it created for growers, slave traders, and associated industries led to one of the most shameful chapters of American history.

Some governments tried to pass new laws against tobacco use. In 1604, King James I of England declared that smoking was "a

custome lothsome to the eye, hatefull to the Nose, harmefull to the braine, dangerous to the Lungs, and in the blacke stinking fume thereof, neerest resembling the
horrible Stigian smoke of the pit that is bottomelesse." In 1631, the Ottoman sultan
Murad IV (1612–1640) decreed that anyone caught smoking would be executed, and,
according to some accounts, as many as fifteen to twenty smokers a day were arrested and put to death. In Russia in 1634, the czar decreed that anyone caught smoking would have his nostrils slit. Similar bans were issued in China, Japan, and India.
But efforts to ban tobacco failed. It was too addictive. By the eighteenth century, it
had become part of cultures throughout much of the world.

Name: Nicotine [NIK-uh-teen]

Source: It's a chemical compound found in tobacco
plants, which are members of the nightshade family (see Atropine Tox Box, p. 54).

Popular poisonous products: Cigarettes, e-cigarettes, snuff, chewing tobacco,
cigars, pipes

How it's delivered: Breathed in, swallowed, chewed, absorbed through the
skin. When tobacco inside a cigarette is burned, it creates a poisonous smoke
that is addictive when inhaled. Tobacco smoke may also contain other poisons,
such as cyanide, hydrogen sulfide, and formaldehyde. Nicotine's toxicity de-
pends on how it enters the body.

Effects: Short-term exposure can cause nausea, vomiting, diarrhea, confusion,
breathing problems, and an irregular heartbeat. Long-term exposure can cause
cancer and heart disease. High doses or direct ingestion may produce vomiting, convulsions, and death.

A medical advice book from 1710 suggests this remedy for headaches:

"Comb Ye Head upwards & stroke it up with nutmeg & vinegar

Take Tobacco

Let Blood in Ye arm or Temple. . . .

Give a vomit"

CHALK IT UP

To adulterate food means to tamper with it. A food adulterer adds stuff to make a product taste better, look better, or cost less to produce. It's almost never good news for the person who eats the food.

The practice has been around ever since people began producing and selling food outside the home. In ancient Greece and Rome, dishonest bakers added chalk to bread. Other food sellers added suspect ingredients to milk, wine, and cheese. In medieval Europe, laws were passed to prevent butchers, bakers, and beer brewers from adulterating their products. In some countries, food adulterers could be put to death.

Food adulteration increased tremendously in Europe and England in the eighteenth century, as more and more

The ingredients were on a knead-to-know basis.

people moved from farms to the cities in search of jobs. They crammed into slums and had no means of preparing their own food, and instead had to rely on food that had been prepared by others—often street vendors.

Profits for food sellers were slim, so it was tempting to swap out expensive ingredients for cheaper ones. And, with few regulations and even less enforcement, adulterating food was easy to get away with. Food manufacturers could—and did—add stomach-turning things to improve the appearance of bad food or replace proper ingredients with cheaper substitutes.

The list of poisons that were eventually discovered in common foods reads like a page torn from a mad scientist's shopping list. Strychnine was added to beer. Sulfuric acid was added to vinegar. Copper salts were put into pickles, wine, and fruit preserves. Lead chromate was added to mustard, wine, and cider. Compounds of copper, lead, and mercury were added to baked goods. Brick dust was added to cayenne pepper. Bright orange Gloucester cheese was colored with red lead. Watered-down milk could be thickened with flour, chalk, plaster of paris—or even snail slime. (The snail slime thickened it up and made a nice froth.) One Italian merchant sold fake Parmesan cheese made from grated umbrella handles. And

some of the most lethal additives of all were added to candy, mostly for bright coloring: mercury sulfide (red), copper carbonate and copper arsenite (green), and lead chromate (yellow).

Honest food sellers were driven out of business by those who undersold them with adulterated products. It's a wonder anyone survived. But, as we'll see in the next chapter, the rise of analytic chemistry helped officials catch many tricksters of the trade.

Name: Strychnine [STRICK-nine]

Source: It's a poisonous chemical most commonly found in the stem, bark, and seeds of the plant *Strychnos nux-vomica*.

How it's delivered: Breathed in, swallowed, or absorbed through the skin

Effects: Strychnine acts fast. When victims swallow strychnine, the poison travels rapidly from the stomach to the blood. The person's muscles clench up rigidly, followed by twitching, frothing at the mouth, and nonstop convulsions of the spinal cord. Often the spasms are so strong that the victim's back arches violently. Even the face contorts.

Strychnine victims often die with a ghastly grin on their faces that is caused by a contraction of the facial muscles. The expression is called *risus sardonicus*, which translates to "mocking smile."

PATENTLY FALSE

It wasn't only food that got tampered with. In the eighteenth century, there was virtually no government regulation of medicines, either. Patent medicines— "remedies" with secret formulas known only to the manufacturers—sprang up for sale all over Europe, England, and eventually America. Anyone could create a product, make wild claims about its surefire cure, and sell it. No medical degree was required. By the end of the eighteenth century, there were more than two hundred elixirs (medicinal potions) and serums offered as treatments

for a host of ailments. Some were downright disgusting: George West's Pectoral Elixir turned out to be made from four gallons each of garden snails and millipedes "bruised to a perfect paste" before being mixed with dozens of other ingredients. William Lowther's Medicinal Compound, supposed to cure epilepsy and worms, contained powdered human skull.

Other products were outright poisonous. One of the better-known cure-alls parents could buy at the pharmacy was Godfrey's Cordial for Children (also called Mother's Friend), for a fussy or teething baby. It contained sinister quantities of opium. Sadly, these products killed many infants.

England's parliament kept voting down legislation that might prevent people from poisoning themselves or others. As a result, anyone could buy dangerous drugs from virtually anyone calling himself a druggist or a chemist.

TOX BOX

Name: Opium [OH-pee-um]

Other names: Laudanum (a solution of alcohol and opium sold as a medicine)

Source: Opium comes from a sticky black substance produced by the seed pods of a poppy plant called *Papaver somniferum,* which is native to the eastern Mediterranean region. Opium contains more than twenty chemical compounds, the most abundant of which is morphine. Today there are many close chemical relatives of opium, produced in a lab and used as powerful painkillers (including heroin).

How it's delivered: Swallowed, injected, snorted, or smoked

Effects: Opium is highly addictive and is a narcotic, meaning it numbs the senses and makes you sleepy. Too much can kill you.

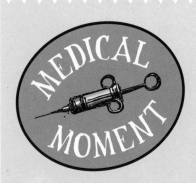

MEDICAL MOMENT

WHEN "GOING" GOT TOUGH, THE TOUGH TOOK MERCURY

Mercury pills and liquid were routinely prescribed for constipation and an upset stomach. Eighteenth-century physicians sometimes instructed their patients to swallow as many as four pints of liquid mercury to dislodge sluggish bowels. Swallowing a hefty handful of lead shot was thought to work well, too. The patient was rolled and jiggled around in an effort to unclog him. With luck, the metal passed through the person and into the chamber pot, unclogging him in the process.

Without luck, patients ended up in worse shape. One man suffering from serious stomach troubles was persuaded to swallow six ounces of lead shot two days in a row. He failed to "pass" the lead pellets and was seized with vomiting, cramps, and "paroxysms." The doctor purged him with "clysters" (see With Friends like These, p. 30), bled him twice (see Medieval Medicine, pp. 38–39), applied twelve leeches to his butt, and dosed him with cherry laurel water (a medicine with cyanide in it) and castor oil. Miraculously, he eventually recovered.

A GOOD, STRONG LOCK KEEPS THE DOCTOR AWAY

In 1711, the forty-nine-year-old eldest son of King Louis XIV of France, also named Louis, caught smallpox. The court doctor, Guy-Crescent Fagon, and his staff went to work trying to cure him. He showed signs of recovering but then suddenly took a turn for the worse and died, most likely from heart failure after prolonged bouts of bleeding, purging, and dosing with poisonous medicines. A few months later, his

younger brother, the next in line to the throne, died of measles, along with his wife. Both of them were also subjected to Fagon's heroic medical treatments. Their two children, boys aged five and two, also caught the illness. After Fagon and his staff worked away on the five-year-old future king, he died, too. Fagon became known as "the killer of princes." The nurse of the two-year-old prince barricaded herself in her chamber with the young child to keep the doctors away from him. He survived and grew up to become Louis XV.

The Duchesse de Ventadour, the royal nurse, is the woman in black on the left, and the young prince she saved, the future Louis XV, is the child in the, er, dress.

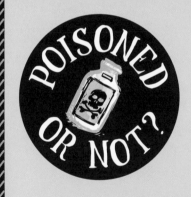

A FEVERISH DEBATE

Ever since his death, in 1791, rumors have swirled that the composer Wolfgang Amadeus Mozart was poisoned by a jealous rival. He himself seems to have been convinced that he was dying of a slow poison and, according to his wife, had mentioned Aqua Toffana (see Drop-Dead Gorgeous, p. 66). In fact, Mozart may have died of acute liver failure. He also may have hastened his own death by taking too much antimony for his fever.

The young Wolfgang Amadeus Mozart.

BAD HEIR DAYS

Poisons in the Nineteenth Century

You can be a famous poisoner or a successful poisoner, but not both.
—Clive Anderson

CROWDED OUT

The Industrial Revolution started in the eighteenth century and continued through-out the nineteenth. It was marked by labor-saving inventions, the rapid growth of

There was no space for a playground on New York City's Mulberry Street.

cities, and remarkable new advancements in the field of science, including in chemistry and medicine. But all that progress created unexpected problems.

Big cities such as London, Beijing, Edo (modern Tokyo), Paris, and New York teemed with new arrivals. The overcrowding strained housing, sanitation, and food supplies. People crammed into filthy neighborhoods, where few had the space or opportunity to cook for themselves, and where toilets and running water were nonexistent. Most felt lucky to find work in factories, even though there were few safety standards. Chimneys churned out black smoke. Epidemic diseases were rampant. Work-related injuries and chronic exposure to poisons became part of the fabric of many people's lives.

WHAT'S MY LINE?

Life was cheap, especially in huge urban centers such as London, which was the biggest city in the Western world in the nineteenth century. If a worker fell ill or suffered an accident on the job, there were ten more people eager to take his place. Often you could tell what a person did for a living by the way he or she looked or acted.

Lead workers were recognizable by their paralyzed wrists, cop-

Breaking up large lumps of coal was a dirty job, but someone had to do it. Unfortunately, the "someones" were usually kids.

per workers by their green-tinted hair and teeth, candy makers by their appalling skin conditions from working with arsenic, and hat makers by their stumbling walk and trembling hands, the result of mercury poisoning (see Nice Work: Hat Maker, p. 94). Painters suffered from painter's colic (see Nice Work: Painter, pp. 60–61), and match makers' jaws were disfigured from exposure to phosphorus (see Nice Work: Match Maker, pp. 92–93).

MATCH MAKER

Gas lighting was invented in the early 1800s. Before that, the only light people could create came from other sources of fire—generally, candles or oil lamps. And, even after gas lighting was invented, most people still used fireplaces to heat their homes.

But think about this: Before matches were invented, it wasn't easy to light a candle. Or an oil lamp. Or to start a fire in the grate. So matches, when they were invented, were extremely useful and valuable. And yet early matches, known as lucifers, had a lot of problems. They flared up unpredictably when struck, and they smelled like rotten eggs. By 1830, match manufacturers began dipping lucifers into white phosphorus (see Tox Box, p. 93), which helped minimize the odor.

A little girl selling matches.

But the coated "safety" matches were also extremely poisonous. There was enough phosphorus in one box of matches to kill a person. Those most in danger of phosphorus poisoning were the people who made the matches.

Workers in match factories, usually women and often children, had different roles, including "mixers," "dippers," and "boxers." Many developed a grisly condition that became known as "phossy jaw." It started with a headache and raging thirst, but after an extended time working with the deadly phosphorus, match makers developed swollen gums, abscesses (pus-filled infected areas),

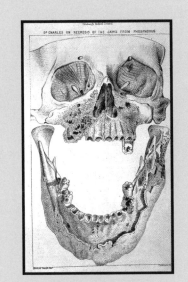

and a gradual disfigurement of the jawbone, which sometimes had to be removed surgically.

Thousands of people in the match industry were poisoned by phosphorus. One reformer in the 1890s gave reporters a dramatic demonstration of the damage when he took them on tours of match makers' homes and turned off the lights. The workers' jaws glowed in the dark.

The skull of a person who had acute phosphorous poisoning——many match makers flamed out quickly.

Name: Phosphorus [FAHS-fur-us]

Source: It's an element (symbol P) found in phosphate rock but also present in trace amounts in urine.

How it's delivered: Breathed in, swallowed, absorbed through the skin

Effects: Long-term exposure to the poisonous versions (white phosphorus and red phosphorus) can cause tissue destruction, particularly of the jawbone. It can also cause loss of appetite, respiratory problems, severe abdominal problems, coma, and death.

HAT MAKER

In the eighteenth and nineteenth centuries, hat making had grown into a booming business in the United States. Everyone agreed that the very-best-quality hats were made from beaver skins, and beavers were plentiful in the New World (for a while, anyway).

The problem was that processing the furry beaver pelts into felt (the woolly part under the outer fur) was dangerous work. Workers had to continually steam and rub the fur in order to remove it. Then, for the next step of the process—creating a fine, matted felt—hatters used poisonous mercury nitrate. They combined mercury with nitric acid, and the danger came from inhaling its vapors. As we know, mercury attacks the central nervous system. Hatters who'd been in the business for a while showed symptoms of chronic exposure: tremors, drooling, muscle weakness, tooth loss, memory loss, and extreme irritability. They also staggered through the streets with an unsteady, "drunken" gait and had trouble talking and thinking clearly. People called

it mad hatter's disease. Lewis Carroll would have known this disease when he created his Mad Hatter character in his 1865 story *Alice's Adventures in Wonderland*.

It wasn't until 1941 that the U.S. Public Health Service finally banned the use of mercury for hat making.

The Hatter, later more popularly called the Mad Hatter, is a famous character in *Alice's Adventures in Wonderland*. The phrase "mad as a hatter" came first and inspired Lewis Carroll's character.

POISON

TOXIC TINTS

One historian has called the nineteenth century the Arsenic Century, and for good reason. In Victorian England, arsenic (see Tox Box, p. 13) seemed to be everywhere. Victorians especially loved the color green. Arsenical green dyes were used in paints, toys, children's books, draperies, wallpaper, and artificial flower leaves. In the days of huge, crinoline hooped skirts, one green muslin gown could require twenty yards of fabric, which, as a medical journal bemoaned, left a waltzer "scattering a dust of poison in the air of a ballroom."

Newspaper accounts recorded death after death from children eating green cake decorations or sleeping in rooms with green wallpaper, where the poisonous color was so loosely attached, you could swipe it off with a napkin. When physicians advised sickly patients to travel to the seashore "to take the air," the patients usually improved, often because they were no longer in a sickroom with green drapery and wallpaper.

Poisoners favored arsenic, too. It was easy to buy, and the symptoms of arsenic poisoning looked a lot like those of cholera. This dreaded disease swept through major cities of the nineteenth century. It caused violent diarrhea and vomiting and could be fatal within hours.

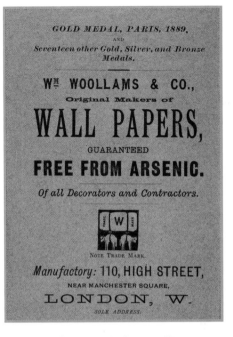

An ad for arsenic-free wallpaper from about 1890. Even then, people knew about the hazards.

POISONED PEPPERMINTS

In 1858, a horrible arsenic poisoning occurred in Yorkshire, England.

The owner of a sweetshop decided to cut costs in his recipe for peppermints, which called for fifty-two pounds of sugar, by swapping in twelve pounds of the much less expensive plaster of paris (calcium sulfate) for some of the sugar.

He sent his errand boy to the next town over to buy the plaster of paris from a pharmacy. The pharmacist, sick in bed, told his own assistant to fill the order. The assistant scooped white powder out of an unlabeled barrel, believing it was plaster of paris. It turned out to be arsenic trioxide.

The powder was mixed into the peppermint drops. The poisoned peppermints killed twenty-one people, many of them children, and sickened more than two hundred before the police, frantically pounding on doors, were able to confiscate the remaining candies. The candy maker, the pharmacist, and the pharmacist's assistant were arrested for manslaughter, but, incredibly, the jury could find no law on the books that said adulteration was illegal. The three were acquitted, but public outrage over the incident sparked more debates in Parliament. Finally, nine years later, acts were passed that limited the sale of poisons only to druggists and chemists.

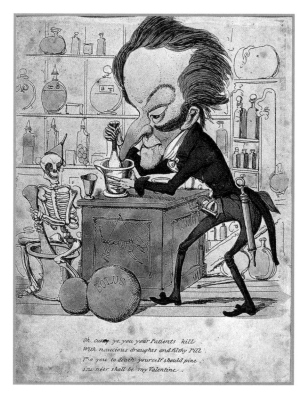

A satirical illustration of an apothecary making a deadly concoction of "naucious draughts and filthy Pill." Note the enema in his holster.

POISONOUS PAPER

Even after the middle of the nineteenth century, when overwhelming medical evidence had convinced most people that green dye posed a hazard, wallpaper manufacturers protested. One producer of popular wallpapers named William Morris swore that his product was safe. (He had inherited a fortune from a family that owned arsenic mines.)

By 1879, Queen Victoria ordered the removal of every bit of green wallpaper from Buckingham Palace. As late as 1885, Morris blamed the poisonous vapors in people's homes on the newfangled flush toilet.

  **POISON**

DEATH BY DECOR

Napoléon Bonaparte (1769–1821) was a military general in France who won many battles and quickly rose to power.

Leaders of other countries in Europe thought he was getting *too* powerful and banded together to try to stop him. His response was to crown himself emperor of France in 1804 and then invade nearly every country in Europe.

In 1812, he suffered a disastrous setback during an invasion of Russia. Thousands of his soldiers died from hunger, cold, and disease, and thousands more died in battle, were wounded, or deserted. Napoléon's empire began to unravel, and in 1814, he was forced to step down. He tried to commit suicide with opium, but it only gave him hiccups and a bout of vomiting, and he recovered.

Napoléon, modestly posing as emperor.

The British sent him to a faraway island off the coast of Italy called Elba, but in 1815, he escaped and returned to power, only to be conquered by the British at the Battle of Waterloo. He was exiled again, this time farther away, to the island of St. Helena, in the middle of the Atlantic Ocean. He lived there for seven years, in chronic ill health, and there he died, convinced he'd been poisoned by his English captors. In his will he declared: "I die before my time, killed by the English oligarchy and its hired assassins."

Was he poisoned? Modern forensic tests show traces of arsenic in his hair. But was he murdered by his British captors, or was he accidentally poisoned by the green-tinted arsenical wallpaper in his sickroom, which would have given off deadly fumes in the damp climate? Most modern historians believe he died of stomach cancer, but some of his symptoms—swollen feet, aching teeth, burning thirst—do sound like those of arsenic poisoning. It may have been cancer that ultimately killed him, but perhaps his death was sped up by an interior decorator.

WHERE THERE'S A WILL, THERE'S A WAY: INSURANCE AND BURIAL CLUBS

One way to measure the overall health of a population is by tracking the rate of infant deaths. And by that indicator, most industrial towns of the nineteenth century were not very healthy. The percentage of babies who did not live to see their first birthday increased over the course of the century—a clear sign that health conditions in crowded cities were declining rather than improving. In London, the most crowded city of all, an average of twenty thousand babies died each year. Infant deaths there reached epidemic proportions between 1846 and 1851.

Many sickly, underfed mothers gave birth too early, and without medical care, the babies quickly died. Many who managed to survive birth perished from damp, cold, bad sanitation, and diarrhea from adulterated food and watered-down milk. Many mothers had to work long hours to make ends meet, and there was no such thing as maternity leave or quality day care. As a result, a whole industry of "baby minders" sprang up. These often-untrained caregivers watched over many children every day and skimped on baby food to save money. Some of them charged lower fees if mothers agreed to allow their children to be dosed with opium or gin to keep them quiet. Many babies died as a result. A grim story—and those were just the accidental deaths.

With so many babies dying, another new industry sprang up, and this one was even more sinister: infant burial clubs. You could join a club for a few cents a week.

THE POOR CHILD'S NURSE.

In this illustration from *Punch* magazine, "the poor child's nurse" is a bottle of opium.

If your child died, the club would pay you enough to cover the funeral expenses, and sometimes quite a bit more. Some parents joined more than one club, which meant if a baby died, they could collect quite a sizable sum of money, by a working person's standards.

Meanwhile, working people could also join "friendly societies," which provided members with money in the event of sickness or unemployment—and paid for funeral expenses, too.

The easy availability of poisons such as arsenic and strychnine (see Tox Box, p. 86), combined with economic desperation and the promise of a large payoff, may well have tempted people to poison members of their own family. And if a cholera epidemic happened to sweep through

The latest style of mourning dress was a popular section in women's fashion magazines.

town, that made things all the easier for a poisoner. The violent convulsions of strychnine deaths could also look a lot like symptoms of certain diseases. Who knows if deaths listed in the official records as apoplexy, epilepsy, diarrhea, cholera, or "fits" might actually have been intentional poisoning?

For middle-class and wealthier people, the new insurance industry was also growing in popularity. The promise of receiving a sizable sum of money when a relative died almost certainly tempted people to poison.

BLOOD, SWEAT, AND SMEARS: THE TRIUMPH OF SCIENCE

By the beginning of the nineteenth century, scientists finally began to win the war against poisoners. Thanks to the efforts of several scientific pioneers, the new field of forensic science was born. As the century unfolded, not only could forensic chemists sometimes detect poison in a corpse, but they were also able to analyze the contents of adulterated foods and suspicious patent medicines and see what possible poisons they contained. Let's meet the Forensic Dream Team.

POISON DETECTIVES

George Pearson (1751–1828): In 1791, this British physician and chemist analyzed the popular patent medicine called Dr. James's Fever Powder. His results proved that that popular "medicine" contained bone ash and the poison antimony.

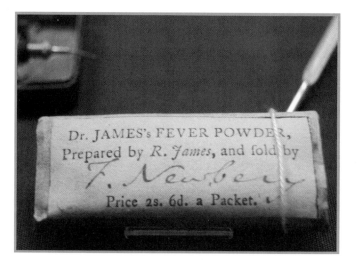

The English physician Robert James claimed that his fever powder, created around 1746, cured all sorts of illnesses. It probably contributed to all sorts of early deaths, too.

Mathieu Orfila (1787–1853): This Spanish chemist is often considered the founder of forensic toxicology. He devoted much of his career to studying arsenic and how to detect it in a corpse. His methods gave detectives an important crime-fighting tool, and he was a key medical expert in many famous criminal poisoning cases.

Frederick Accum (1769–1838): This German chemist fought against food adulteration from his lab in London in the early nineteenth century. He analyzed popular products to show what they contained. Then, in 1820, he published his book, listing the names and addresses of known food adulterers. Included among his examples of adulterated foods: red lead, used to color cheese; sulfuric acid, added to vinegar; and all sorts of ingredients mixed with bread flour—including alum, or plaster of paris, or even sawdust. He revealed that some candies were colored with green arsenic. The public was outraged, and the first edition of his book sold out in a month. But Accum, not surprisingly, also made a great many enemies. In 1821, one of them accused him of a petty theft. In disgrace, he moved back to Germany. Soon his book was forgotten, and it would be thirty more years before the British government passed laws to stop the practice of adulterating food.

James Marsh (1794–1846): In 1836, British chemist James Marsh developed a groundbreaking test that could find even the smallest trace of arsenic in a dead body. His method was to cut tissue from a dead body and add zinc and sulfuric acid to it inside a glass tube. If arsenic was present, a chemical reaction would occur, and when heated, a silvery-black coating would appear on the inside of the tube. The Marsh test became the primary way to determine the outcome of

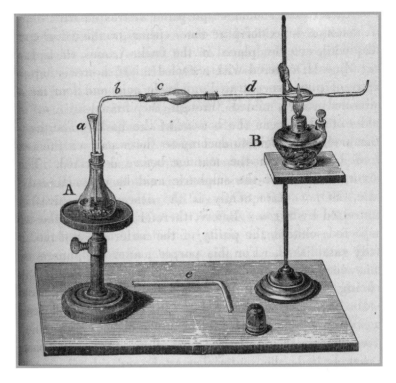

The Marsh test.

arsenic murder trials for the rest of the century and was the first use of toxicology in a jury trial.

Jean Servais Stas (1813–1891): With the success of the Marsh test, arsenic poisonings declined. But poisonings by strychnine, morphine, and nicotine, which were thought to be untraceable in a body, began to rise. Then, in 1851, for the very first time, a Belgian chemist named Jean Servais Stas developed a test that could identify traces of nicotine in the body of a murder victim.

In a very public and sensational murder trial, Stas proved that the victim, Gustave Fougnies, had been poisoned by his assassins, Count Hippolyte Visart de Bocarmé and his sister. They had held him down and poured distilled liquid nicotine down his throat, followed by vinegar, to hide the smell. Stas's test for nicotine was improved upon five years later, and versions of it could also be used to detect strychnine.

TRYING TO PLAN THE PERFECT CRIME?

Sir Robert Christison (1797–1882) was a famous toxicologist and a professor at the University of Edinburgh, and was often used as an expert witness in murder cases. Once, during the cross-examination in a murder case, he was asked whether there might be a "perfect poison," one that couldn't be detected in a dead body. Christison turned to the judge and reportedly said, "My Lord, there is but one deadly agent of this kind which we cannot satisfactorily trace in the human body after death, and that is—"

Here the judge interrupted him, saying, "Stop, stop, please, Dr. Christison. It is much better that the public should not know it."

Christison was later reported to have revealed the poison in a lecture, when he declared that what he was going to say, be-

fore the judge interrupted him, was that the perfect, most undetectable poison was aconite, commonly known as monkshood or wolfsbane (see Aconite Tox Box, p. 104). But don't get any ideas. Thanks to modern forensics, that poison can very much be traced in a dead body.

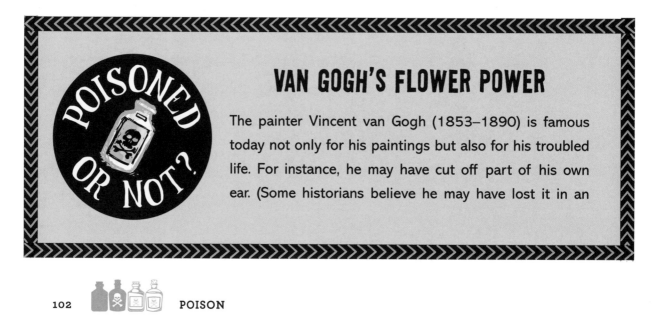

POISONED OR NOT?

VAN GOGH'S FLOWER POWER

The painter Vincent van Gogh (1853–1890) is famous today not only for his paintings but also for his troubled life. For instance, he may have cut off part of his own ear. (Some historians believe he may have lost it in an argument with his frenemy, the artist Paul Gauguin.) Theories that explain his strange behavior include side effects of epilepsy, bipolar disorder, vertigo, too much absinthe (a powerful alcoholic beverage that contains the poisonous chemical thujone), and lead poisoning from his toxic box of paints (see Nice Work: Painter, pp. 60–61). One thing is certain: he loved the color yellow. His house was painted yellow. Most of his paintings in his later years were dominated by yellow.

His doctor, Paul-Ferdinand Gachet, may have treated Van Gogh for epilepsy with

digitalis, extracted from the foxglove plant. Digitalis was a common medicine at the time (and a form of it is still used today). It was also used as a sedative.

One of the known side effects of treatment with digitalis is that it makes you see heightened yellows and greens and causes the world to look as though you're seeing it through yellow-tinted sunglasses. The two portraits that Van Gogh painted of his doctor both show him holding a foxglove flower. Coincidence?

Many of Van Gogh's most famous paintings featured sunflowers and other sun-drenched scenes.

Name: Aconite [ACK-uh-nite]

Other names: Aconitine, wolfsbane, leopard's bane, dog's bane, devil's helmet, and monkshood

Source: Aconite is a genus of plant (*Aconitum*), a member of the buttercup family. There are over 250 kinds of *Aconitum* plants, and most contain the poison aconitine.

How it's delivered: Absorbed through the skin or swallowed

Effects: Burning of the mouth, nausea, vomiting, diarrhea, constriction of the throat, dizziness, blindness, and a sense of doom. High doses can cause death.

TOXIC TONICS

The business of advertising and selling patent medicines grew into a booming business in Europe and America in the nineteenth century. The cost of printing plunged, and because school was becoming required for everyone, more and more people could read—and they bought newspapers. The new railroads delivered mail cheaply and quickly, so patent medicines could be advertised and delivered by post.

In England, Fowler's Solution was popular for treating epilepsy, skin disorders, and syphilis (see Fowler's: Not the Best Solution, p. 105). Charles Darwin took it regularly. So did the novelist Jane Austen.

In the United States, popular patent medicines included Professor Low's Liniment & Worm Syrup,

Advertisements and labels could say anything—and they did.

Dalley's Magical Pain Extractor, Dr. Kilmer's Swamp Root, Hood's Sarsaparilla, Wistar's Balsam of Wild Cherry, Dr. King's New Discovery, Edgar's Cathartic Confection, Schenck's Mandrake Pills, and Pinkham's Vegetable Compound for Female Weakness.

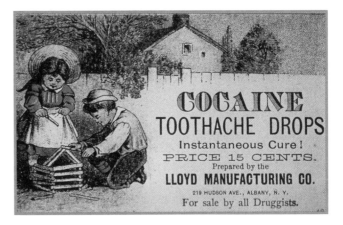

No, this is not a product from a joke shop.

At best, the patent medicines were useless. At worst, they were dangerous poisons. Most were some combination of sugar, alcohol, and opiates. With no laws to stop them, companies made wildly fraudulent claims for cures and didn't list their ingredients.

FOWLER'S: NOT THE BEST SOLUTION

Introduced in the 1780s by Dr. Thomas Fowler, Fowler's Solution was a combination of arsenic trioxide, alcohol, and lavender water. Doctors prescribed it for a host of ailments, including indigestion, nausea, flatulence (gas), and eczema (a skin condition). It became extremely popular and was found in many households' medicine cabinets. People rubbed it into their hair to kill lice. Women sipped it to improve their complexions. People even believed it worked as an aphrodisiac (love potion). In the short term, it may have been effective for treating various ailments. In the long term, it could give the patient cancer. It remained on pharmacy shelves as late as the 1950s.

THE MUSE

Elizabeth Siddal (1829–1862) was a famous beauty and an artist's model who eventually became the wife of painter-poet Dante Gabriel Rossetti. She led a distinctly unhealthy lifestyle. She was addicted to laudanum (a mixture of opium and alcohol, available over the counter in those days). She also took daily doses of Fowler's Solution to maintain her smooth complexion. In 1862, she took too much laudanum and died. Her distraught husband had her buried along with the only copy of his manuscript of poems, which he placed in her coffin.

Elizabeth Siddal, posing in one of her many emo portraits.

Seven years after his wife's death, he had a change of heart. He wanted his poems back. He was granted permission to have her body dug up. Witnesses who saw the opening of her coffin said her body was remarkably well preserved, most likely due to the arsenic she'd taken in the form of her daily dose of Fowler's Solution (see Fowler's: Not the Best Solution, p. 105).

STEP RIGHT UP: SNAKE-OIL SALESMEN

Nowadays, describing a product as snake oil is a way of saying it's a phony medicine that promises to do something that it can't. But in fact, the original snake oil, one of the most common cure-alls of the nineteenth century, actually may have worked.

When Chinese laborers came to the United States in the 1860s to help build the transcontinental railroad, they brought with them a special ointment for sore, achy muscles. It was made from the

Chinese water snake, *Enhydris chinensis*. They probably shared it with their American coworkers. Word spread that the stuff worked.

When a modern neurophysiology researcher analyzed the snake oil, he discovered that the oil contains omega-3 fatty acids that soothe inflammation in muscles and joints.

The term "snake oil salesman" came to mean "dishonest person" after some American patent-medicine makers made their own versions of snake oil. Some peddled elixirs made from rattlesnakes. Rattlesnake oil doesn't have as high a concentration of omega-3 fatty acids as Chinese water snake oil, but Chinese water snakes were scarce in the American West. Some con artists peddled snake oil that contained no snake products whatsoever.

MEDICAL ROAD SHOWS

Nineteenth-century American patent-medicine salesmen traveled from town to town selling their phony medicines and putting on carnival-like medicine shows. Between comic monologues, banjo solos, and card tricks, they would demonstrate how well their medicines worked, usually by "healing" members of the audience who were actually their accomplices and in on the scam. After convincing the audience and selling their wares, the hucksters would quickly leave town, before people realized the worthlessness of the products they'd purchased.

THE OPIUM WARS

Opium had been used as a medicine in China for hundreds of years, but with the introduction in the seventeenth century of the tobacco pipe, the Chinese realized that mixing tobacco with Indian opium could be a potent way to become intoxicated—and it was extremely addictive. At first, smoking opium was a relatively expensive habit, reserved mostly for the wealthy. But by the beginning of the eighteenth century, it had become a widespread problem, and in 1729, the emperor banned opium smoking.

That was when the problems with Britain began. China also happened to produce most of the world's tea, and people in eighteenth-century Britain wanted more and more of it. Britain had little to trade that interested the Chinese. So the British had to buy Chinese tea with silver. And the British didn't want to part with their silver. So British traders hit upon another idea. Because the British controlled much of India, where opium was grown, the British East India Company had access to lots of opium. The East India Company would increase the demand for opium in China. That way, China would trade tea for opium instead of silver.

British traders dumped thousands of pounds of opium into the Chinese market, hoping to drop the price of opium and get more Chinese people addicted. The plan worked. More and more Chinese people could afford to buy it and did so. Opium addiction in China soared.

Alarmed, the Chinese imperial court passed new, stern laws to ban opium use and importation.

An opium den customer.

So a bustling smuggling trade sprang up. In 1839, the Chinese petitioned Victoria, the queen of England, to help put a stop to the smuggling. She ignored the request.

When the Chinese seized twenty thousand barrels of opium at a Chinese port, the British declared war and attacked the port city of Canton. That was the first of the two Opium Wars (1839–1842 and 1856–1860). Britain won, and China was forced to pay huge fines, to open its ports to trading, to hand over control of Hong Kong to Britain, and ultimately to legalize opium in China. Many British businessmen grew extremely wealthy. A few Americans grabbed a piece of the action, too. German-born American businessman John Jacob Astor became the first American multimillionaire through trading in opium.

THAT PALE NINETEENTH-CENTURY COMPLEXION— GET THE LOOK!

Want to achieve that deathly white pallor that's so in with the Victorian crowd? Nope, can't use makeup—respectable nineteenth-century women don't paint their faces. But nibbling on an arsenic wafer will give you that corpse-like look. But be careful not to eat too many, or you'll end up a *real* corpse.

Dreadful detail: many of those nineteenth-century patent creams that claimed to tighten the chin, erase freckles, or whiten the complexion also contained high levels of arsenic.

FEELING FIZZY

Coca-Cola and 7UP

Many people in the eighteenth and nineteenth centuries believed that naturally occurring fizzy mineral waters were healthful to drink. So beverage manufacturers thought it would be profitable to try to create fizzy water in the laboratory. In 1767, chemist Joseph Priestley managed to add a bit of fizz to still water. Using fermented yeast, he was able to add carbon dioxide to make a weak, bubbly drink. But the water lost its fizz quickly.

By 1832, chemists created a sturdier fizz, but efficient bottling methods hadn't been invented yet. Soda fountains appeared in many pharmacies. In the days when many medicines were delivered in liquid form, the sweet-tasting soda could mask bitter medicines such as quinine. Early ads for sodas touted them as a healthy way to start the day off right.

Coke—a favorite nineteenth-century pick-me-up—had more than just caffeine in it.

Pharmacists created energy drinks—soda mixtures with drugs they called nervines, which included strychnine, cannabis, morphine, opium, heroin, and cocaine, newly discovered in 1855. Although the doses were small, they must have had quite an energetic, not to say addictive, effect. The men who made the drinks were called soda jerks because of the jerking arm movement needed to operate the machinery.

A soda jerk—he could make a milk shake with real get-up-and-go.

Coca-Cola was concocted and first advertised in 1886 and was sold as a health drink. The *coca* part of the name came from the coca plant (which contains cocaine), and the *cola* part came from the African kola nut, which has a high caffeine content. By 1903, the company had removed cocaine from the drink.

The drink you know as 7UP was originally called Lithiated Lemon Soda. It contained lithium citrate, a mood enhancer, well into the 1950s.

Early 7UP for Depression-era depression.

A DOPEY DISCOVERY

In 1874, a scientist named C. R. Alder Wright at St. Mary's hospital in London began experimenting with morphine. He added an extra chemical to it and created diacetylmorphine. By 1898, the German drug company Bayer began marketing the drug as Heroin, then a trademark. Bayer's Heroin was hailed as a superaspirin and marketed as a cough suppressant and headache remedy. It was soon found to be highly addictive and was taken off the market in most countries.

9

TWENTIETH-CENTURY TOX

In a democratic country the ballot, after all, is the determining factor,
the solution of a grave public health menace.
—Dr. Charles Norris, chief medical examiner, New York City

ANALYZE THIS

With the arrival of the twentieth century, the nature of poisoning began to shift. At last, chemists had mostly outpaced poisoners. Poisons were also more difficult to buy at the local drugstore.

Over the course of the twentieth century, the sale of poisons became more strictly regulated. But poison didn't go away. It just changed.

There were now fewer instances of lone assassins slipping cyanide into someone's soup. The new villains—crooked manufacturers, greedy businessmen, and negligent industrialists— were far more interested in profit than public health and worker safety. Poisons continued to harm people on the job, to find their way into food and medicine, and to wreak havoc on the environment. Incidents of poisoning on a large scale happened with greater frequency.

UNRULY AND UNREGULATED

Although people knew about food adulteration and dangerous patent medicines, pre–twentieth century lawmakers in Europe and America had not done much to regulate the problems. Newspapers reported on the issues, the public was outraged, and laws were passed—but fines were low, and enforcement was uneven.

Thanks to Theodore Roosevelt (who was president from 1901 to 1909), the tide began to turn. He hired a new head of the Bureau of Chemistry of the U.S. Department of Agriculture (which would later become the Food and Drug Administration), who unleashed a team of chemists to conduct investigations. They

We'll try anything!

The Poison Squad.

found that a lot of the food sold in the United States had been chemically adulterated. From 1902 to 1906, they enlisted a group of twelve volunteers. Nicknamed the Poison Squad, their job was to ingest food and drink that had been laced with common preservatives, including borax and formaldehyde. Each man was monitored for any "evil change in his physical condition." They embraced their task and even came up with a toast:

Oh, here's to good old germs,
Drink 'em down!
With their scientific terms
Drink 'em down!

For the poison wine squad placid
Drinking salicylic acid
Fears no microscopic worms—
Drink 'em down!

In 1905 and 1906, *Collier's* magazine ran a series of scathing articles called "The Great American Fraud," denouncing patent-medicine manufacturers as crooks who often sold poisonous products.

And then, in 1906, journalist Upton Sinclair published a novel called *The Jungle*. His intention was to shine a light on the miserable working conditions of the mostly Polish and Lithuanian immigrants who produced and handled meat. But his descriptions of the Chicago stockyards horrified his readers. Together the *Collier's* articles and Sinclair's book raised widespread awareness. The public demanded changes.

The book that horrified a nation.

On June 30, 1906, President Theodore Roosevelt signed into law the Pure Food and Drug Act.

Used for good . . . and evil.

THE BUTLER DID IT

By the early twentieth century, chloroform was commonly used to ease the pain of surgery. But it wasn't long before criminals discovered that it could be used for dark purposes. A victim could be rendered unconscious by having a rag soaked with the liquid held over the mouth.

In 1901, the philanthropist William Marsh Rice was killed by his valet, who'd been bribed by a crooked lawyer planning to benefit from a forged will. The valet used chloroform on his employer while he was sleeping. The crime was discovered, and Rice's fortune eventually founded Rice University, in Texas.

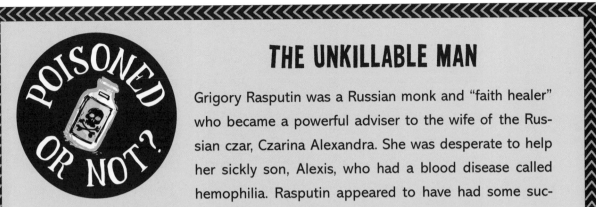

THE UNKILLABLE MAN

Grigory Rasputin was a Russian monk and "faith healer" who became a powerful adviser to the wife of the Russian czar, Czarina Alexandra. She was desperate to help her sickly son, Alexis, who had a blood disease called hemophilia. Rasputin appeared to have had some success in helping the boy through bouts of illness. But the Russian nobility hated Rasputin, who came from a humble background and had immense psychological power over the royal family. Several members of the nobility hatched a plan to murder him.

On a cold December night in 1916, Rasputin was lured to the home of one of the conspirators, where he was fed chocolate cake and wine that had been heavily laced with cyanide. To the conspirators' horror, Rasputin appeared to suffer no ill effects. In desperation, one of them shot him in the back. He fell down as though dead but then sat up, bellowing. They shot him three more times and then bludgeoned him over the head with a heavy object, just to make sure he was truly dead. They dumped his seemingly lifeless body into a hole in the frozen river.

If looks could heal.

Rasputin.

When his very-dead body was eventually fished out, an autopsy was performed. No trace of cyanide could be found in his remains. Had the person who'd been entrusted with the task of putting the poison into his food chickened out? Rumors swirled that he'd regained consciousness and managed to free his tied hands after he'd been dumped into the water. (This seems unlikely, as there was no water in his lungs, indicating he'd not been breathing when he'd entered the water.) The specific details may never be known.

PROHIBITION AND ALL THAT JAZZ

In 1919, the United States Congress ratified an amendment to the Constitution. The Eighteenth Amendment banned the manufacture, sale, and transportation of alcoholic beverages. It ushered in a period of American history called Prohibition. On January 17, 1920, the new amendment went into effect.

What a dump—police pouring out illegal liquor.

Almost immediately, people began making and selling illegal liquor. They were called bootleggers. Customers flocked to drink the bootleg alcohol at illegal drinking spots called speakeasies. Ironically, Americans seemed to be drinking more during Prohibition than they had before. Criminal activity and violent crimes increased. So did the rates of alcoholism.

THE DRINKABLE AND THE UNTHINKABLE-TO-DRINK

Ethyl alcohol is the drinkable kind of alcohol that you find in liquor. Humans have been making it for thousands of years by fermenting grain, fruits, and vegetables.

Methyl alcohol, also known as methanol or wood alcohol, is a common byproduct of industries that produce wood products and charcoal. Nowadays it's made synthetically. It has many legitimate uses, including in antifreeze, paints, cosmetics, and rocket fuel, but it is poisonous if you drink it.

Industrial alcohol is ethyl alcohol that has been denatured, or mixed with chemicals—often including methyl alcohol—in order to make it unfit to drink. Back in 1906, the U.S. government ruled that manufacturers had to denature their alcohol to avoid paying the high taxes imposed on drinkable alcohol. So manufacturers added extra chemicals to their industrial alcohol to make it taste terrible, and many of the chemicals they added were poisonous.

TOXIC COCKTAILS

As soon as Prohibition went into effect and alcohol was banned as a beverage, bootleggers began stealing industrial alcohol. The chemists who worked for the bootleggers were paid better than the law-abiding chemists, and they figured out how to redistill the industrial alcohol to remove most of the poison.

In 1923, a synthetic form of methyl alcohol was invented, and it was added to industrial alcohol. Bootleggers stole that, too. People continued to mix the bootlegged alcohol into their cocktails, and many got sick. It made them vomit, feel dizzy, and bump into stuff. Some people went blind. Others died.

Furious that the anti-alcohol laws were being ignored, officials of the U.S. government responded by requiring that more and more poisonous chemicals be added to industrial alcohol. Their reasoning? It would taste so disgusting, people wouldn't drink it. Wrong. Bootleggers kept using it. People kept drinking it. People kept dying.

The story gets crazier and crazier. The response by the U.S. government was to make alcohol *so poisonous and awful tasting,* no one could *possibly* be idiotic enough to drink it. Additives included nicotine, kerosene, gasoline, mercury, aniline, benzene, formaldehyde, and cyanide. The so-called denatured alcohol was more poisonous than ever, but bootleggers figured out ways to "renature" it and make it drinkable—sort of.

In 1926, as many as twelve hundred people in New York City were blinded or sickened by drinking poisonous alcohol. An additional four hundred died.

Garters were handy for holding up your stockings—and for stashing a flask.

Poorer people, who couldn't afford the higher-priced and relatively less toxic alcohol, tended to fall ill or die more frequently. "The desire to obtain some kind of drink leads persons of the poorer classes to resort to almost any kind of drink containing alcohol, such as tincture of iodine, alcoholic solution of shellac, canned fuel, alcohol for anti-freezing, &c," reported New York City's chief medical examiner, Charles Norris. Across the country, tens of thousands of people were blinded, paralyzed, or killed by drinking poisoned alcohol.

A great debate arose. On one side were those who thought Prohibition was a complete disaster that should be repealed. They pointed to the rise of violent crime syndicates, the increased rates of alcoholism, and the alarming death tolls. On the opposing side were those in favor of continuing Prohibition. They argued that alcohol use was the cause of many terrible social problems and that it was the government's duty to abolish it. They also argued that if people were dumb enough to drink poisoned alcohol and then died, well, it was their own fault. They thought the government should take even stronger action to poison the alcohol supply and crack down on bootlegging.

By the early 1930s, most people sided with the anti-Prohibitionists. One of the campaign promises of Franklin Roosevelt was that he would overturn Prohibition. He was elected president in 1932. By September 1933, enough states had voted to bring back legal alcohol that Prohibition came to an end.

KNOCK-KNOCK

Henry Ford's Model T rolled off the assembly line in 1908 and quickly became the first widely produced automobile in the United States. Other manufacturers soon followed.

The engines in early automobiles had an unnerving tendency to emit loud banging noises under the hood, known as knocking. The noise was the result of inefficient combustion (burning). Because the gasoline wasn't completely burned away by the engine, traces

of gasoline tended to heat up and explode, sounding like a gunshot. In 1921, an engineer at General Motors tried adding lead (technically tetraethyl lead, or TEL) to the gasoline, which cured the knocking problem. In May 1923, the new fuel was used by several drivers in the Indianapolis 500. The first three finishers all ran on gasoline containing TEL.

People have known the dangers of lead since ancient Roman days, and lead executives knew that it was hazardous. But, they reasoned, wasn't a little bit of lead exposure the price society had to pay in the interest of progress? Just what was an "acceptable level" of lead exposure?

In 1924, GM, together with its part owner DuPont, formed an alliance with Standard Oil and created the Ethyl Corporation. They called their TEL-containing gasoline Ethyl gas. It sounded much nicer to use the word "ethyl" than "lead." Advertisements for Ethyl often showed an attractive woman (presumably named Ethyl). No mention of lead appeared anywhere.

Would you buy deadly lead from this lovely lady? A lot of people did.

But before long, workers at the Standard Oil TEL processing plant in New Jersey began behaving oddly. Their mental deterioration—a result of inhaling the lead-filled vapors—became evident as they grew moody and forgetful and showed strangely erratic behavior, such as trying to brush phantom insects off their arms. They collapsed, grew delirious, and twitched. Workers in other areas of the company dubbed the place where these people worked the "looney gas building." After two months, thirty-two of the forty-nine workers were hospitalized, and five died—some of them screaming in straitjackets. The Public Health Service made an inquiry. The politically powerful oil companies insisted that the workers had simply worked too hard. But after two workers at a DuPont TEL processing plant also died, the plants were ordered shut down.

Standard Oil held a press conference. They brought in the original developer of TEL, Thomas Midgley Jr., who insisted to reporters that TEL was safe. So safe, in fact, that he washed his hands in the stuff right in front of them. A few months later, he sought medical treatment for lead poisoning.

A government task force was appointed, but it was stacked with pro–oil industry scientists. In a statement issued in January 1926, the Public Health Service report determined that TEL was safe so long as workers wore protective clothing. The report concluded that there was no reason to prohibit the sale of leaded gasoline.

The Ethyl Corporation manufactured TEL until 1985. Leaded gasoline used to fuel cars was not phased out completely until 1996.

TAINTED PAINT

As more and more American families moved from the country to the city in the 1920s, more and more children were exposed to lead. Lead was in gasoline and also in foil candy wrappers, cake dyes, toys, cribs, and, especially, in paint.

In 1928, the politically powerful lead industry began a vast marketing and public-relations campaign to create a positive image for lead paint, much the way it was doing with Ethyl gasoline. As a result, the general public wasn't made aware of the true dangers of lead paint for young children for decades. It wasn't until the mid-1950s that several brave scientists risked damaging their careers to call attention to the danger. More and more articles began appearing in scientific journals, warning of the

This cute little blond boy became the face of Dutch Boy lead paint—which ironically poisoned a lot of children.

dangers of lead. One study noted that a single two-inch-square chip of lead paint would be enough to kill a small child who ate it.

The lead industry continued to insist that poisoning by lead paint was not a wide-

spread problem and that kids who were poisoned by paint chips had poorly educated parents who didn't pay enough attention to their unruly children. But the negative publicity mounted. In 1971, President Nixon signed the Lead-Based Paint Poisoning Prevention Act, and further amendments in 1973 and 1976 lowered the acceptable lead content in paint.

CRIMES OF THE CENTURY

In 2010, the incidence of violent crimes in the United States hit a near-fifty-year low. The worst year for violent crimes had been 1980.

Why has the crime rate dropped? What is our modern society doing right? Do we have better law enforcement? Longer jail terms? Better parenting? Or could the cause be something completely different?

What if we looked at lead exposure? Is a child who is exposed to lead more likely to grow up to become a criminal? Did toddlers who ingested high levels of lead in the 1940s, 1950s, and 1960s grow up to commit violent crimes in the 1960s, 1970s, and 1980s? Is there a direct correlation between the drop in violent crime statistics and the removal of lead from paint and gasoline? According to the results of a recent study, the answer to all of these questions is yes.

We now know that even low doses of lead exposure can lead to neurobehavioral problems. In other words, it can muddle your thinking and make you do really dumb things like commit crimes. In a study by the Centers for Disease Control and Prevention, the percentage of U.S. children with elevated blood lead levels dropped from 88.2 percent in the 1970s to 4.4 percent by 1995.

Numerous studies have shown that high blood lead levels result in lower IQs. In other words, reducing a child's exposure to lead can raise that child's intelligence. Can less lead also be linked to a drop in violent crime? It's an intriguing theory.

PUBLIC HEALTH HERO

One of the unsung heroes of public health is an American scientist named Clair Cameron Patterson (1922–1995). He first warned of the dangers of lead in the environment in 1959, and for the next decade, he campaigned tirelessly for the removal of lead from paint, gasoline, and canned food. He encountered strong opposition from the lead and oil industries and from scientists employed by those industries. They claimed

Clair Patterson.

Hero without a cape.

that the lead in the environment occurred naturally. Patterson proved that much of it was the result of human-made products. In 1966, he spoke before a U.S. Senate special hearing about the environment. His testimony and meticulous research helped usher in the passage of the Clean Air Act of 1970.

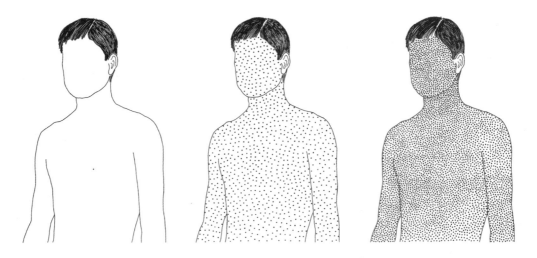

An alarming graphic from Dr. Patterson's research comparing the lead levels that would have been found in the body of a prehistoric person (left), those of a modern person living in an industrialized area (middle), and the amount of lead necessary to cause classical lead poisoning (right).

MISLED ABOUT LEAD

Lead remains a continuing problem in many communities. In 2002, tests showed that schools in the city of Camden, New Jersey, contained high lead levels in its water. Almost fifteen years later, Camden schools were still relying on bottled drinking water. In 2016, Newark, New Jersey, officials turned off the water in thirty schools due to high lead levels. Meanwhile, in Flint, Michigan, city officials admitted that political decisions and efforts to cut costs had exposed thousands of people to dangerous lead levels in the drinking water.

You won't want to drink this water.

Flint, Michigan

Marie and Pierre Curie in their lab.

NONE LIKE IT HOT

In 1898, a new metallic element was discovered by physicist Marie Curie and her husband, Pierre. They called the new element polonium (see Tox Box, p. 148), after her native country, Poland. That same year, they discovered and named the element radium (see Tox Box, p. 126). The Curies had to refine several tons of a material called pitchblende to obtain tiny amounts of radium. Along with the recently discovered element uranium, these became known as radioactive elements.

SCIENTIST

Those "mad scientist" characters you've seen in cartoons and science fiction movies may have some basis in reality. In the early days of experimentation in the laboratory, alchemists worked with dangerous substances, including mercury and lead. And even as alchemy gave way to natural philosophy and then to science and chemistry, many scientists, like the alchemists before them, poisoned themselves while working in unventilated laboratories with toxic materials. Some famous examples:

- **Isaac Newton** (1642–1727): The scientist who developed the principles of modern physics was also an alchemist. He probably poisoned himself with lead and mercury fumes in the laboratory. He suffered from insomnia, loss of appetite, delusions, and memory loss, all of which are symptoms of mercury poisoning. When twentieth-century scientists analyzed a hair sample of his, they found that it had greatly elevated levels of mercury, lead, arsenic, and antimony.

- **Carl** (sometimes spelled Karl) **Wilhelm Scheele** (1742–1786): In 1778, he concocted a dye made from copper arsenite and called it Scheele's green (see Nice Work: Painter, pp. 60–61). In 1782, he isolated hydrogen cyanide, also called Prussic acid. He had the bad habit of smelling and tasting his chemicals. He became an invalid at thirty-five, most likely from heavy-metal exposure, and died at forty-three. His symptoms seem to fit with classic mercury poisoning.

- **Robert Bunsen** (1811–1899): The German chemist, after whom the Bunsen burner is named, worked with arsenic compounds, which he claimed made him hallucinate and caused his tongue to turn black. During one experiment, a beaker of cacodyl cyanide exploded and permanently blinded him in one eye.

- **Marie Curie** (1867–1934): The discoverer (with her husband) of radium and polonium died of a cancer related to radiation poisoning. In 1956, her daughter Irène Joliot-Curie, also an esteemed scientist, died at fifty-eight of leukemia, probably the result of her work with radioactive material.

- **Karen Wetterhahn** (1948–1997): In 1996, the cancer research scientist was working with a compound called dimethyl mercury, a dangerous poison, when a drop of the substance fell onto her gloved hand. The chemical can easily pass through a latex glove, and it did so. Five months later, she developed symptoms of mercury poisoning: an unsteady gait, slurred speech, and impaired eyesight. She slipped into a coma and died.

Name: Radium [RAY-dee-um]

Source: It's an element with the chemical symbol Ra that occurs naturally in the earth's crust.

How it's delivered: Breathed in, swallowed, or absorbed through the skin

Popular poisonous products: Skin creams, health drinks, glow-in-the-dark watches

Effects: Radium is radioactive. That means it isn't stable, and decays into a stable state, throwing off high-energy particles that can mess with your body's normal chemistry. Depending on the amount of radiation received, symptoms can include nausea, vomiting, diarrhea, burns to the skin, bleeding, hair loss, and eventually infertility, brittle bones, cancer, and death.

THE RADIUM GIRLS

By the turn of the twentieth century, physicians had discovered that low doses of radium shrink cancer tumors in some patients. Radium grew in fame and was touted as a miracle cure for all sorts of ills, including rheumatism, dandruff, low energy, and "dull teeth." It became a common ingredient in patent medicines. People drank

Radium girls at work.

radium water, smoothed radium facial creams on their skin, applied luminous radium lipstick, and even sucked on radium lollipops.

During World War I (1914–1918), airplane dials were painted with glow-in-the-dark paint made from radium, and glow-in-the-dark watches were developed for soldiers so that they could see what time it was in the darkened trenches. After the war, glow-in-the-dark watches became all the rage. Several watch-dial-painting factories sprang up. "Radium girls," mostly young women with keen eyesight and nimble fingers, painted luminous numbers on watch dials with radium-based paint, at eight cents a dial. They were taught to lick the tips of their brushes to get a pointier tip. Many did so hundreds of times a day. It was considered a good job, with

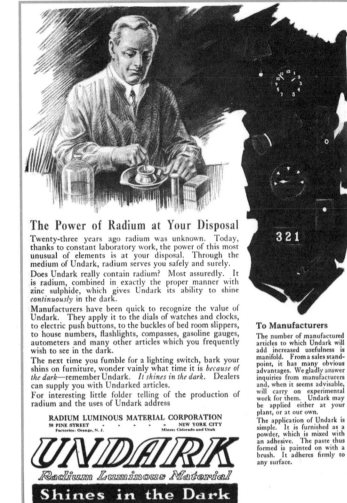

Radium—the power to make any watch glow in the dark.

good pay and clean working conditions. Just for fun, the young women decorated their fingernails and teeth with the luminous substance. Consumers could even buy it over the counter in order to paint their own watch faces. The product was called Undark.

What no one realized was that the radium was poisonous. Soon the workers began to grow sick. Their teeth fell out, their jaws cracked, and their bones broke—sometimes when they merely rolled over in bed. Several died. The watch company denied that radium was the reason. Even scientists and medical authorities were convinced that radium was "liquid sunshine," and they suggested the girls' illness was the result of impurities in the radium paint rather than the radium itself.

It wasn't until 1932, when a famous millionaire died of radiation poisoning, that people realized that downing radioactive liquid for lunch was not such a great idea. The public's belief in the health benefits of radium abruptly ended.

Some of the radium girls who'd gotten sick were given a lump-sum settlement of $10,000, and the company paid for their medical bills. But many others received no compensation at all and died in extreme pain.

RADIATING HEALTH: FOR A WHILE

In 1928, a wealthy American socialite, athlete, and businessman named Eben Byers visited a well-known doctor, complaining of aches and pains and a general run-down feeling. The doctor suggested he try a patent medicine called Radithor. The radium-laced "wonder drug" had been introduced in 1925 by a man named William J. A. Bailey. His company, Bailey Radium Laboratories, ran ads that guaranteed that Radithor was "harmless in every respect."

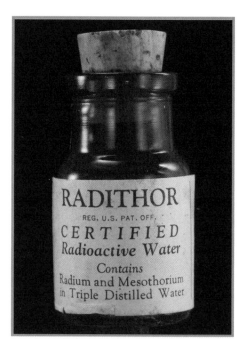

Byers drank several bottles of Radithor a day. At a dollar a bottle, the medicine was expensive (this was the 1920s), but he claimed it made him feel energetic and healthy, and he recommended it to many of his wealthy friends.

About two years after he began taking the Radithor, Byers visited his private physician. Byers had lost weight and was having headaches and dental problems. He reported that he'd lost "that toned up feeling." When his teeth started falling out, consultants were called in. Their diagnosis confirmed what his physician suspected: Byers was suffering from radiation poisoning.

By 1931, Byers was very sick. After two operations, he'd had most of his jaw removed, and holes were forming in his skull. He died in 1932.

The public was shocked by the news of his death. Despite some troubling reports of deaths in a few watch-painting factories, everyone still believed that radium water was a health tonic. Even James Walker, the mayor of New York City, admitted to taking radioactive rejuvenating medicines.

An investigation into Bailey Radium Laboratories was begun. When officials from the Newark City Health Office tried to contact Bailey, they found he had left town. Bailey was never prosecuted for anything serious because the laws pertaining to patent medicines at the time had little power to protect consumers.

EVIL ELIXIR

During the 1930s, sulfanilamide was a drug commonly used to treat streptococcal infections and had been used safely for some time in tablet and powder form. But salesmen for the Massengill Company in Bristol, Tennessee, asked for a liquid form of the drug. A company chemist and pharmacist, Harold Cole Watkins, experimented and found that sulfanilamide would dissolve in diethylene glycol. He added some raspberry flavoring, which gave it a pretty pink color as well as a pleasing, sweet taste. The company shipped 240 gallons of the product, called Elixir Sulfanilamide, all over the country.

Diethylene glycol is used in antifreeze and brake fluid. It's also used in cosmetics and household products, as a solvent for paints and plastics, and as a softening agent for cellophane. It creates the artificial smoke and mist in theatrical productions.

Just a spoonful of . . . poison?

(Some Broadway performers have suffered headaches and dizziness after repeated performances involving artificial smoke.) And all the glycols and their compounds (that includes **eth-**, **dieth-**, poly**eth**ylene) are deadly poisons if you ingest them.

At the time, food and drug laws did not require that safety studies be done on new drugs. People began dying, and most were children, who'd been given the medicine for their sore throats. Victims suffered symptoms characteristic of kidney failure—severe abdominal cramps, nausea, vomiting, convulsions—and intense pain.

It didn't take long to determine that Elixir Sulfanilamide was the cause of the deaths. FDA agents fanned out across the country, trying to retrieve the elixir. In many drugstores, it had been sold without a prescription to people the druggists didn't know.

The incident hastened the enactment, in 1938, of the Federal Food, Drug, and Cosmetic Act.

Although the Massengill Company refused to assume responsibility for the incident, Harold Cole Watkins, the company pharmacist who'd concocted the elixir, committed suicide soon after learning the results of his invention.

TOXIC COSMETICS

In 1933, a woman was rushed to the hospital after using an eyelash-darkening treatment called Lash Lure. It contained a toxic coal-tar dye. The woman went blind.

In the 1930s, a number of people suffered from baldness, pain, and paralysis after using a cream for hair-removal called Koremlu. The product contained thallium (see Tox Box, p. 131). The U.S. government had no power to ban poisonous cosmetics until the 1938 act was passed.

It gave the FDA some power, but—some people argued—not enough. Cosmetics continued to contain lead, mercury, formaldehyde, and other dangerous chemicals.

Too high a price to pay to be beautiful.

Name: Thallium [THAL-ee-um]

Source: It's a soft metallic element with the chemical symbol Tl. Thallium is found in certain minerals and is a by-product of producing sulfuric acid, and also of mining lead or zinc.

How it's delivered: Swallowed, or absorbed through the skin. A fatal dose for an adult is less than a quarter of a teaspoon.

Popular poisonous products: Once used as a hair-removal cream

Effects: Abdominal pain, nausea, vomiting, and diarrhea, as well as lethargy (lack of energy), numb hands and feet, slurred speech, and a frozen face that leaves the victim unable to move his mouth or speak. In the case of chronic poisoning, the hair falls out after ten to fourteen days, and telltale lines appear on the fingernails. Delirium, seizures, and twitching may set in, followed by death.

PATRIOTIC PUFFING

By the mid-1850s, cigarette smoking became more popular than pipe smoking in the Ottoman Empire (now modern Turkey). British soldiers fighting in the Crimean War (1853–1856) learned about cigarettes from their Turkish allies and brought them back to England. The smoker had to roll each cigarette individually.

Cigarettes in the United States didn't become popular until after the Civil War (1861–1865). Before that, people took tobacco through pipe smoking and in the form of chewing tobacco and snuff. An efficient cigarette-making machine was invented in the 1880s, which meant that cigarettes no longer had to be rolled by hand and could be cheaply produced.

There were attempts to ban smoking in the United States in the early 1900s—not so much for health reasons as for moral ones. (For the same reasons, there were also attempts to ban dancing, drinking, and gambling.) In 1908, New York City banned women from smoking in public. (That law

didn't last long.) In a shrewd marketing move, the tobacco companies provided fighting forces in World War I with free cigarettes. As a result, many soldiers came home addicted to cigarettes, and bans on smoking seemed unpatriotic. Tobacco companies did the same thing in World War II (1939–1945; the United States entered in 1941), which meant that a new generation of soldiers returned from war addicted to cigarettes. By 1965, *42 percent* of American adults smoked.

But health concerns were growing. Two major reports were issued (in Britain in 1962, and in the United States in 1964) that linked smoking to cancer. Although the tobacco industry continued to deny the accusations that smoking was unhealthy, television smoking ads were banned in 1969, and cigarette smoking at last began to decline.

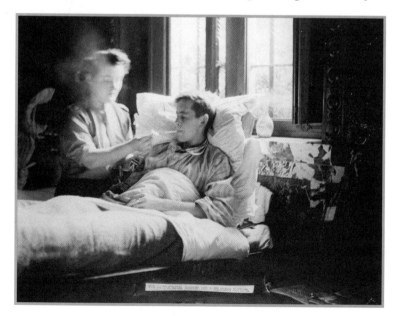

Cigarettes were once considered the best medicine.

Could nicotine (see Tox Box, p. 83) be the most tragic and deadly poison in this whole book? It has caused a lot of human misery: the demand

for tobacco led directly to millions of African slaves being brought to North America. And the death statistics become almost numbing: One hundred million people died worldwide from tobacco-related diseases in the twentieth century. Each year, smoking-related illnesses kill four hundred thousand Americans. As tobacco companies continue to develop smoking markets in other parts of the world, there's the potential for millions more deaths in the twenty-first century.

ASTHMA CIGARETTES? YES, REALLY

Asthma cigarettes containing jimsonweed (*Datura stramonium*) were marketed under the name Asthmador and were thought to help treat asthma, coughs, tuberculosis, and bronchitis. Some doctors thought jimsonweed had an antispasmodic effect—that is, they believed it could relax muscles and prevent a patient's lungs from narrowing painfully. By the mid–twentieth century, other doctors challenged the notion that smoking anything was a good idea for people with asthma, but the powerful tobacco companies continued to run ads that claimed that "medicated" cigarettes were beneficial to people with respiratory troubles.

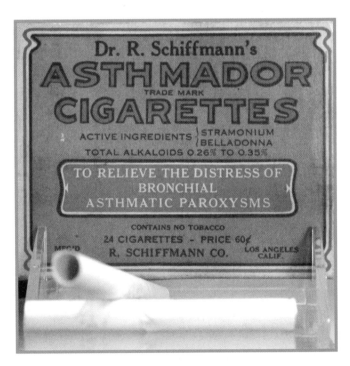

Asthma cigarettes were sold as late as the 1960s. Yet the popular belief that herbal cigarettes may have health benefits persisted. When tobacco companies added menthol to cigarettes, their ads claimed that the minty taste soothed the throat and made smoking a smoother experience. But the result was that smokers inhaled more deeply. Today about one-fourth of all cigarettes sold are mentholated.

Smoking to relieve asthma?
Do not try this at home.

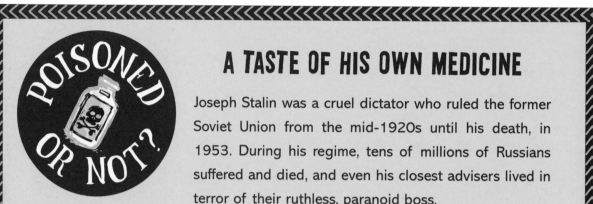

A TASTE OF HIS OWN MEDICINE

Joseph Stalin was a cruel dictator who ruled the former Soviet Union from the mid-1920s until his death, in 1953. During his regime, tens of millions of Russians suffered and died, and even his closest advisers lived in terror of their ruthless, paranoid boss.

In 1953, he collapsed after an all-night dinner with four members of his inner circle. When he did not emerge from his room the next day, his staff grew alarmed. But no one was allowed to enter his private chambers unless they were summoned. Finally, at 11 p.m. members of his panicked staff entered and found Stalin lying on the floor.

He died four days later, officially of a brain hemorrhage. But recently, long-secret Soviet documents have come to light that suggest he may have been poisoned by one of the dinner guests, all of whom had reason to fear for their lives.

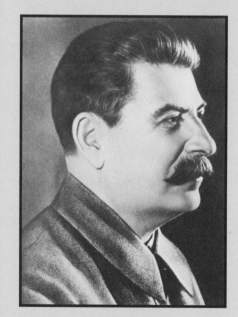

Joseph Stalin, about 1942.

Stalin may have been poisoned by warfarin, a medicine still in use today as a blood thinner for people with heart problems. It's also used as a rat killer. The tasteless, colorless substance may have been slipped into his wine at dinner.

The original report revealed that Stalin had vomited blood, suggesting stomach bleeding. Warfarin would cause stomach bleeding. A brain hemorrhage would not. The stomach-bleeding detail was deleted from the official medical report released to the public at the time of his death.

KILLING CASTRO (NOT)

Fidel Castro (1926–2016) became the leader of Cuba in 1959. In the opinion of many members of the U.S. government, he was a tyrant and a dictator, and because he allied himself with the then-Communist Soviet Union, he became an official enemy of America. Almost as soon as Castro assumed power, the U.S. government began secret efforts to get rid of him.

Castro was known for always appearing in his military uniform, with a bushy beard and his signature cigar. Between 1959 and 1965, there

Fidel Castro, 1959.

were at least eight plots by the U.S. Central Intelligence Agency to either assassinate him or make him look like such a bad leader, his own Cuban people would want to overthrow him. During his long career, the CIA planned *hundreds* of attempts to get rid of him. Some never got beyond the discussion stage. The plots weren't uncovered until 1975, when a Senate investigation made some of them public.

Poison was a key weapon in many of the CIA's plots, which included a plan to smuggle cigars laced with botulinum (see Tox Box, p. 136) into Castro's house, to deliver a skin-diving suit dusted on the inside with poison, and to put thallium into his

shoes. The idea was that the thallium would make his beard fall off and would damage his image. Castro learned of some of the plots and took great delight in reporting that none of the attempts succeeded.

Castro stepped down as president of Cuba in 2008, at the age of eighty-one, after ruling for nearly fifty years. He died of natural causes in 2016.

Name: Botulinum [bot-choo-LIH-num]

Source: Botulinum is a powerful toxin produced by the bacterium *Clostridium botulinum,* which is usually found naturally in the soil. It causes the illness known as botulism.

How it's delivered: Swallowed, injected, absorbed through the skin. Infants can get botulism from honey, but we're not quite sure how.

Effects: Slurred speech and muscle weakness. Left untreated, botulism can lead to paralysis, inability to breathe, and death. When administered by a qualified physician, botulinum can be used for certain medical conditions, such as painful neck contractions, jaw clenching, crossed eyes, and headaches. It blocks chemical signals sent from nerves that cause muscles to contract.

THE UMBRELLA MURDER

In 1971, the writer Georgi Markov defected from his native Bulgaria and settled in London. On a British radio station, he broadcasted back to his homeland stories that were critical of the Communist Bulgarian regime. This clearly angered Bulgarian officials. At the time, people in Bulgaria were not free to voice criticisms of the government.

On Thursday, September 7, 1978, Markov was standing at a bus stop in London when he felt a jab in his thigh. A stranger with a folded-up umbrella muttered an apology and hurried away. By the next morning, Markov was in the hospital with a high fever. His white-blood-cell count soared, and by Monday he was dead.

An autopsy was performed. Inside the puncture wound in his thigh, doctors found a pinhead-sized pellet with two tiny holes in it. It had been fired into Markov's thigh by the umbrella gun. After much testing and analysis of Markov's symptoms, the experts concluded that he had been poisoned by ricin (see Tox Box, p. 138).

Although all signs pointed to the Bulgarian secret service, many of the papers pertaining to the incident were destroyed, and the man believed to have been in command of the plot died in a mysterious car accident. The case was never solved.

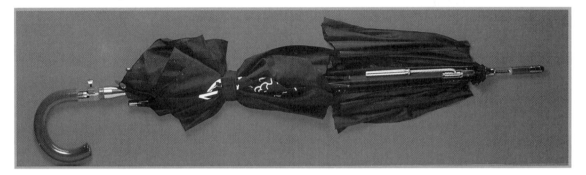

In 1978, the KGB used an umbrella like this—modified to fire a tiny pellet filled with poison—to assassinate dissident Georgi Markov on the streets of London.

CULT SHOCK

On November 18, 1978, more than nine hundred members of a religious cult called the Peoples Temple, living in Guyana, a country in South America, committed suicide or were murdered. The poison they took, or were forced to take, was cyanide-laced fruit punch.

The cult leader was a man named Jim Jones. He was a skilled preacher and lured almost a thousand people to the

Jim Jones in a photo taken about a year before the tragic Jonestown mass suicides.

South American jungle to live in an "ideal" community, which he modestly named Jonestown. But he demanded loyalty and obedience from his followers. He coerced or brainwashed many of them into signing over all their possessions and convinced them that terrible things would happen to them if they left the cult. Several times he staged rehearsals for a mass suicide.

When a U.S. congressman named Leo Ryan flew to Guyana with a team of investigators, Jones ordered that Ryan's group be assassinated. Ryan was shot and killed, along with several members of the press. Other members of the investigation team managed to get away. Fearing that those who had escaped would return with authorities, Jones ordered the temple members to carry out their suicide plan. Jones himself died of a gunshot wound.

Name: Ricin [RICE-in]

Source: Ricin is a poison found inside the seeds of the castor-oil plant (*Ricinus communus*) and other related plants.

How it's delivered: Breathed in, swallowed, or injected. If injected in its purest form, ricin is twice as deadly as cobra venom and five hundred times more toxic than arsenic or cyanide.

Effects: Heavy sweating, difficulty breathing. The skin might turn blue. If it's injected, the victim experiences vomiting, diarrhea, hallucinations, and seizures. Organs begin to shut down, and death may occur in three to five days.

BOTOX—GET THE LOOK!

The botulinum toxin is one of the most fearful poisons known. So why not inject it into your face? The toxin freezes up the muscles, makes wrinkles relax, and helps remove those pesky frown lines. The paralysis can last up to a year.

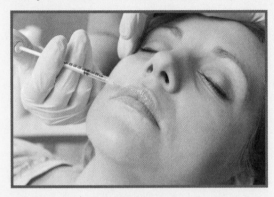

Beauty hurts.

DROP-DEAD GORGEOUS

BAD THINGS COME IN SMALL PACKAGES

In 1982, seven people in the Chicago area were killed when they took Tylenol capsules that had been laced with cyanide. The nation went on high alert. Investigators determined that the cyanide had been added to the bottles after they'd left the factory.

The poisoner must have taken bottles off the shelves at local drugstores, added the poison, and then returned them to the shelves. The murderer was never found. But manufacturers quickly developed tamper-proof packaging, which today has become standard.

SARIN IN THE SUBWAY

In March 1995, more than five thousand people in Tokyo were sickened by a poisonous-gas attack on the Tokyo subway. The poison unleashed by the attackers was called sarin (see Tox Box, p. 141). Twelve people died.

A shadowy cult called Aum Shinrikyo was responsible for the attack. Its leader, Shoko Asahara, had convinced his followers that the end of the world was coming, and he thought he'd hurry things along with a chemical attack in the subway. Evidently he believed the ensuing panic might destabilize the government and lead to a third world war. Or something.

On the morning of the attack, five cult members entered the subway with small plastic bags of liquid sarin. Each carried a sharpened umbrella. At the peak of rush hour, the attackers pierced the bags with their umbrellas and immediately exited the

First responders after the sarin attack in a Tokyo subway.

POISON

train. The poison leaked out and quickly evaporated to form a deadly vapor, which caused train riders to begin to cough and vomit.

Police swiftly traced the attack to the cult and arrested most of the people responsible. Three remained fugitives for another decade or so but were eventually caught.

Name: Sarin [SAR-in]. It's a combination of the names of the four scientists who developed it: Schrader, Ambros, Rüdiger, and van der Linde.

Source: Sarin is a human-made chemical, produced in the laboratory, and is not found naturally in the environment. It was created as a pesticide.

How it's delivered: Swallowed, breathed in, absorbed through the skin or through contact with the eyes. It vaporizes easily.

Effects: Within seconds of exposure, victims may experience eye pain, blurred vision, drooling, sweating, nausea, and confusion. Large doses may result in unconsciousness, convulsions, paralysis, and death. The good news is, people with a mild exposure usually recover completely.

NEW AND NOXIOUS

Poisons in the Twenty-First Century and Beyond

Let us learn from the past to profit by the present, and from the present, to live better in the future.
—William Wordsworth

WICKED WEAPONS

With modern times come modern perils. Our ability to detect poisons is better than ever, and yet those intent on using poison to harm others have also gotten more sophisticated. We'll open this chapter with several modern mysteries, famous twenty-first-century poisoning cases.

DEATH BY POST

In September 2001, just after the terrorist attacks of September 11, in New York and Washington, D.C., letters containing deadly anthrax spores were mailed to several news media organizations and to the offices of two U.S. senators in Washington, D.C. The poisoner had used a specially made, "weaponized" form of anthrax that was deadly if a person inhaled even a tiny amount of it (see Tox Box, p. 144). Five people were killed and seventeen more were sickened. The Senate offices shut down, the postal system was paralyzed, and much of the country panicked. Were there more letters out there? Who had sent them? No one claimed responsibility.

A thorough investigation took place, but it wasn't until 2008 that a suspect was identified. However, the suspect was already dead.

The dead suspect was named Bruce Ivins. He had been a biodefense researcher at the U.S. Army Medical Research Institute of Infectious Diseases. He had apparently committed suicide from an overdose of Tylenol. (There was no suicide note.) He had been deeply involved in anthrax research. Evidence against him was mostly circumstantial (that is, there was no physical proof), yet federal prosecutors declared that he was the person responsible, and the case was closed.

But some scientists and journalists were not convinced that Ivins was the anthrax killer. They pointed to the fact that the anthrax that had been used had been dried, aerosolized, and coated with silicon ("weaponized"), which made it vaporize when the letters were opened. The skeptics claimed that Ivins had neither the equipment nor the know-how to attach the silicon to the anthrax he worked with. The true story remains a mystery.

First responders decontaminating one another outside the Senate office building after the anthrax attacks.

Name: Anthrax [AN-thraks]

Source: Anthrax is an illness caused by the bacterium *Bacillus anthracis*. The bacterium produces an extremely lethal batch of poisons called anthrax toxin. Anthrax spores are present in the soil, and the illness affects livestock and wild animals that eat or inhale the spores while grazing. Humans can become infected by direct contact with sick animals. Anthrax spores have been "weaponized" in the laboratory and used as a deadly poison.

How it's delivered: Swallowed, breathed in, absorbed through the skin

Effects: Flu-like symptoms, skin sores, vomiting, shock, delirium, and death. Often symptoms don't develop for seven days after exposure. Grisly detail: the toxin causes cells in your immune system to explode, which can lead to septic shock and death.

SCARRED FOR LIFE

Viktor Yushchenko was the president of Ukraine from 2005 to 2010. But before he was president—during his campaign in 2004—he fell seriously ill. Yushchenko claimed that someone had tried to poison him. He accused his political opponent, Viktor Yanukovych. The Yanukovych supporters scoffed at Yushchenko's accusation and blamed him for eating bad sushi and drinking too much cognac.

Eventually doctors came to agree with Yushchenko. After running many tests, they determined that he had, indeed, been poisoned and that the poison that had been used was dioxin (see Tox Box, p. 145). He suffered severe abdominal and back pain, and the left side of his face was paralyzed. Over time, his face began to show signs of lesions and blisters. His skin was left permanently scarred, but he survived.

Dioxins are difficult poisons to trace. A single drop in Yushchenko's food could have made him sick without his even tasting it. How it got there was never determined.

Before (left) and after (right) pictures of Yushchenko, taken four years apart. You can clearly see the effects of scarring on his face.

Name: Dioxin [dye-OX-in]

Source: Dioxins are a group of chemically related compounds, usually environmental pollutants created as by-products of industrial processes, but they can also result from natural processes such as volcanoes and forest fires. Dioxins have been synthesized and used as poison.

How it's delivered: Swallowed, breathed in

Effects: Short-term exposure may result in skin lesions and problems with liver function. Long-term exposure can impair the body's immune, nervous, endocrine, and reproductive systems. Victims have an increased risk of cancer and death.

YOU'VE GOT SNAIL

Researchers have recently discovered a promising new painkiller that's a thousand times more powerful than morphine but isn't addictive. The source? A venomous snail, *Conus magus*, that lives in coral reefs in the Pacific Ocean. It uses its long, flexible proboscis (a tubelike projection) to harpoon fish, worms, and other snails, which it then injects with paralyzing venom. Larger cone snails have enough venom to kill a person. In 2004, the FDA approved the use of

a synthetic drug called Prialt to treat patients suffering from severe and chronic pain. It contains a toxin identical to that found in the cone snail venom. Because it has to be injected into the spine, it's not yet in widespread use.

SECRET ASSASSINS

Here's another case that reads like a spy thriller.

In November 2006, a man in a London bar met up with two mysterious companions. All three appeared to be Russians. The waiter served the first man a pot of green tea, and the others multiple rounds of gin. After the men had left, the waiter cleared the table. He noticed that the tea he poured into the sink had a gooey consistency.

Two days later, the man who'd ordered the tea was rushed to the hospital. His name was Alexander Litvinenko. Vomiting and growing ever sicker, he insisted he

had been poisoned. His hair soon began to fall out.

More than two weeks after he'd fallen ill, doctors reached the conclusion that he was right, and that the poison was thallium. But they were wrong about the thallium. Litvinenko got sicker and sicker, and three weeks after having drunk the poisoned tea, he died. After more testing, the doctors discovered that the poison that

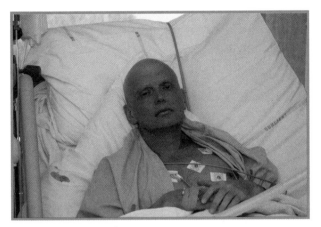

Litvinenko, only days before his death.

had killed Litvinenko was the extremely rare and extremely radioactive polonium-210 (see Tox Box, p. 148).

Litvinenko had published a book in 2002 accusing Vladimir Putin, then the leader of the KGB, or the Russian secret service, of bombing some Moscow apartment buildings in 1999. Litvinenko claimed that Putin had blamed the bombings on Chechen rebels in order to justify an assault on the Chechens, and that Putin's actions had eventually helped Putin get elected president. After Litvinenko's death, it was revealed that Litvinenko had been a spy working for British intelligence. His death was considered a political assassination. It was one in a series of mysterious fatal poisonings of Russian dissidents. (A dissident is a person who speaks out against his or her own government.)

Forensic investigators wearing protective suits were able to follow a radioactive trail taken by Litvinenko from the time he left the bar where he'd met the two agents, to the hotel kitchen, where the waiter had poured out the toxic tea, to the car he'd driven home. The radioactive trail was painstakingly decontaminated. (The waiter survived—polonium-210 is deadly if swallowed or inhaled, but it can't poison you if you get some on your skin.)

British investigators were also able to follow another radioactive trail—the one left by the KGB assassins. They tracked it from aircrafts to hotels to the seats the assassins had occupied in a soccer stadium. The trail led them all the way back to Russia and to the two suspects. But the Russian government refused to turn the men over to British investigators.

Name: Polonium [puh-LOH-nee-um]

Source: It's an element with the chemical symbol Po that occurs naturally in the earth's crust in trace amounts.

How it's delivered: Swallowed, breathed in, or absorbed through a cut in the skin

Effects: Like radium, polonium is radioactive. Symptoms can include nausea, vomiting, diarrhea, burns to the skin, bleeding, and hair loss. Just a speck of dust-sized amount of polonium is highly poisonous if swallowed, absorbed, or breathed in. Once inside the body, radioactive particles bombard the internal organs and kill off cells rapidly. By the time the poison enters the bone marrow, the lymphatic system shuts down. Death follows.

WAY TO GLOW

In the former East Germany, the secret police, known as the Stasi, were believed to have secretly tagged dissidents with radioactive chemicals so that they could be tracked with Geiger counters. Up until the Communist East German state collapsed, in 1989, as many as a thousand dissidents may have been tagged.

The cheerful-looking Stasi headquarters in the former East Berlin.

ARAFAT'S LAST DAYS

In 2004, the Palestinian leader Yasser Arafat began vomiting several hours after eating dinner. Four weeks later, he died in a French military hospital. French doctors announced that the cause of death was a massive stroke. No autopsy was performed.

Yasser Arafat.

Almost immediately, rumors began circulating that he had been poisoned. Then, eight years after his death, a bag of his belongings that had been given to his widow shortly after his death was delivered to a news agency. The contents were analyzed and were found to be emitting radiation. But, since no one knew where the belongings had been for those eight years, they could have been contaminated after Arafat's death. In 2013, the body was exhumed (dug up), and scientists from Switzerland performed forensic tests on it. They announced that they had found traces of polonium in the remains that were eighteen times higher than normal. A year later, in 2014, French scientists rejected the suggestion of intentional poisoning and announced that the level of polonium in the body was naturally occurring.

Was he poisoned, or was his death due to natural causes? Certainly there were many people who wanted to get rid of him. We may never know for certain, but we do know that only three countries are known to be able to reliably produce polonium: Russia, the United States, and Israel.

TESTING, TESTING

Today, computers do much of the analysis in toxicology labs, and testing can be much quicker and more reliable than it used to be. Gone are the days when investigators rubbed stuff on rabbits, fed stuff to dogs, and tasted victims' bodily fluids. Modern-style tests for toxins include chromatography, infrared spectroscopy, mass spectrometry, atomic absorption spectrometry (AAS), neutron activation analysis (NAA), and energy-dispersive X-ray fluorescence (SEM-EDX). Modern forensic scientists can now take a kind of "molecular fingerprint" that allows the tester to see what substances might be present in a sample.

Toxicology ROCKS! (No, really.)

And yet, despite the way it may appear on TV, the job of detecting poison is still not a foolproof science. Testing for unusual or exotic poisons can be expensive and time consuming. With eight million chemical compounds on earth, even the best lab tests don't always find poison if it happens to be one of the rare ones. Successful results are often based on skill, intuition, and just plain luck.

POISONS PAST AND FUTURE

The history of poison highlights both the best and the worst sides of human nature.

So let's look at the bright side. Think of the scientists, and the alchemists and herbalists before them, who sacrificed their health, and sometimes their lives, in the quest to discover plants and minerals that paved the way for modern medicine.

Be grateful for the reformers, who fought to protect the health of workers and the public and the environment. They're the reason we have regulations in place to protect us. Nowadays you don't have to try to cure a sore throat by chewing on a leaf you found in your backyard and hoping for the best. You can walk into a drugstore and buy something in an attractive, sterile package, and you can feel pretty confident that it's been tested and approved by qualified professionals.

But the dark side of the story has not gone away. Poisoners still lurk, plotting dark deeds or higher profits for themselves. We still hear stories in the news about crooked manufacturers who adulterate foods and household products. People still get poisoned on the job. And even many medicines and painkillers that play an important part in fighting disease and lessening pain can be extremely dangerous and addictive if used the wrong way.

What's the best way to protect yourself from modern-style poisons? It would be impractical for you to hire a poison taster, and tough for your social life if you walked

around in a hazmat suit. But you *can* appreciate the need for regulations that protect the public and the environment. You can appreciate poison control centers that help protect us from accidental poisoning, and brave scientists and public health advocates who continue to stand up for what's best for us. You can read the ingredients on food labels; it's a good rule of thumb that the fewer additives, the better. And you can read labels on household products carefully and follow the safety precautions. Most important of all, you can consider a career in medicine, toxicology, forensics, law enforcement, or environmental science.

And, just to be on the safe side, watch out for people wearing rings with secret compartments or carrying pointy-tipped umbrellas.

ACKNOWLEDGMENTS

There are many people who gave me support, advice, and guidance as I researched this book. Thanks to Professor Mary Smith at Cornell University for spending the better part of a day giving me a tour of the poisonous plants garden and sharing with me her vast knowledge of plants, and to Brian Spatola, collections manager of the Anatomical Division at the National Museum of Health and Medicine, who also devoted many hours to showing me fascinating specimens from the museum's collections. Thanks to Amber Paranick at the Library of Congress, Danielle Aloia at the New York Academy of Medicine, Patti Taylor at the Taft School, and Melissa Grafe at the Yale Medical Library, for helping me dig up facts, images, and primary sources I never would have found otherwise. Thanks to William Lamb and Jacqueline Carroll Hanratty, (grown) children of radium girls, who graciously answered my questions about their mothers' experiences. Thanks to the members of the science department at the Taft School, especially Jim Lehner, Laura Monti, and Amanda Benedict, for reading portions of the manuscript and answering my incessant science questions. Big thanks to Laura Sanman, a PhD candidate in chemical and systems biology at the Stanford School of Medicine, for her help with the Tox Boxes, glossary, and general chemistry questions. Any errors that may have occurred are mine and mine alone. Special thanks to the many, many reference librarians—best friends of nonfiction writers—for their ongoing assistance in helping me track down sources, particularly at libraries in Darien, East Hampton, Southampton, Bridgehampton, and West Hartford, and at Yale University, the New York Public Library, the New York Academy of Medicine, the Library of Congress, the National Archives, and the Taft School. Thanks to my trusted readers, Michaela Muntean, Marcia DeSanctis, and Cassie Willson, for reviewing and editing early incarnations of the manuscript, and to writer friends Erin Dionne, Loree Burns, and Kate Messner for their many excellent suggestions. Huge thanks to Karl Edwards for his hilarious illustrations, and to my awesome agent, Caryn Wiseman, for her wisdom and encouragement. My deep gratitude to everyone at Crown, especially Emily Easton, Samantha Gentry, Nicole Gastonguay, Stephanie Moss, and the entire team at Random House Children's Books.

Also a big thank-you to all my Nerdy Book Club educator friends, old and new, for their infectious and boundless love for books, authors, and illustrators.

And, of course, love and gratitude to my husband and kids for putting up with all the gruesome dinner-table talk.

GLOSSARY

addictive: habit-forming

adulterant: an inferior and sometimes dangerous ingredient

alchemy: a medieval pseudoscience that aimed to change base metals into gold and to discover an elixir that would prolong life

alkaloid: a naturally occurring chemical compound that is produced by living things (usually plants) and that contains nitrogen. Alkaloids can be fragrant, bitter, or poisonous and have been used as drugs, medicines, and poisons.

analgesic: a substance that relieves pain

antidote: a substance that counteracts or interrupts the effects of a poison

aphrodisiac: a love potion; a drug or food that arouses passion

apothecary: a pharmacist or pharmacy; someone who prepares and sells medicines

astrology: the study of planets and other celestial bodies and their supposed influence on human affairs

atom: a single unit of an element

autopsy: an examination of a dead body to determine the cause of death

bezoar: a stony substance from the stomach of an animal, thought to ward off poison

cantharides: a poison made from ground-up blister beetles

ceruse: an old-fashioned term for a white-lead pigment, often used as makeup

chemical: anything with a distinct composition of molecules that is produced by or used in a chemical process

chemical compound: When atoms bond, they form a molecule. If at least two of the atoms are different elements, it is a chemical compound.

clyster: see *enema*

combustion: burning

dioxin: a poison; one of a class of chemicals usually formed by burning hydrocarbons and chlorine

element: a substance made of atoms that have an identical number of protons in each nucleus

elixir: a medicine, usually combined with a sweetener, alcohol, and water

elixir of life: a substance believed to cure all ailments or make you live forever

emetic: a substance that causes vomiting

enema: a liquid introduced into a person's rear end for medicinal or health reasons, usually to bring on a bowel movement. Also called a clyster.

forensic toxicology: a discipline of chemistry that studies poisons and other toxic substances as an aid to medical or legal investigations into poisoning

laxative: a food or drug that stimulates the bowels (i.e., makes a person poop)

mineral: a naturally occurring substance that is usually solid and inorganic and that has a crystal structure. It's different from rock, which doesn't have a regular chemical composition and which can be a combination of minerals and nonminerals.

mithridate: an ancient concoction used as a poison antidote, named after Mithridates

molecule: two or more atoms held together by chemical forces

narcotic: an addictive drug that reduces pain, alters mood, and brings on sleep or numbness

opiate: any one of a group of drugs that are derived from opium or from chemicals that resemble opium, and that have a sedative (calming) effect

ore: a kind of rock that contains specific elements and minerals that can be extracted

orpiment: a bright yellow arsenic sulfide ore, once used as a paint

paralysis: loss of sensation (feeling) in a part of the body; an inability to move

philosopher's stone: a substance believed to be able to change a base metal into gold

poison: a substance that causes harm by means of a chemical action in the body, especially one that causes harm in small doses

radioactive: emitting radiation (alpha particles, electrons, or gamma rays)

realgar: a red arsenic sulfide ore, once used as a paint color

scarification: a process of making shallow cuts in the skin

sedative: a drug that has a soothing effect

smuggling: importing or exporting something unlawfully

snake oil: a preparation that is peddled as a cure for a variety of illnesses and that is usually not effective

stibnite: an antimony ore, once used as a cosmetic

toxic: capable of causing injury or death, usually by chemical means; poisonous

toxicant: a poison that is either human-made or is the result of human activity

toxicology: the study of poison

toxin: a poisonous chemical produced by plants, animals, or microorganisms

venom: a fluid that contains toxins and is produced by an animal

venomous: of or relating to an animal that delivers poison by biting, stinging, or secreting

vesicant: a chemical compound that causes blisters and severe irritation

A HISTORY OF MODERN POISONS AND PUBLIC HEALTH REGULATIONS IN THE UNITED STATES

1906: The Pure Food and Drug Act is passed and is signed into law by President Theodore Roosevelt. The act prohibits the selling of adulterated or misbranded drugs and requires labeling of dangerous or addictive substances. But it does not regulate cosmetics or medical devices. The Meat Inspection Act is also passed.

1907: The first Certified Color Regulations lists seven colors that are suitable for use in foods.

1923: Leaded gas is introduced into the market.

1930: The Food, Drug, and Insecticide Administration's name is shortened to the Food and Drug Administration. The FDA is responsible for protecting public health.

1938: The Federal Food, Drug, and Cosmetic Act is passed in response to the Sulfanilamide disaster (see pp. 129–130). Among other things, the new law brings cosmetics and medical devices under FDA control. Also, it requires that companies prove to the FDA that new drugs are safe before they can be advertised, and that they be properly labeled.

1941: The U.S. Public Health Service bans the use of mercury in hat making.

1941: The FDA identifies more than twenty dangerous drugs that can be sold only by prescription.

1953: The first Poison Control Center opens, in Chicago. Five years later, there are seventeen Poison Control Centers in the United States.

1964: The surgeon general's report links lung cancer to smoking.

1965: Congress passes the Federal Cigarette Labeling and Advertising Act, which requires the following surgeon general's warning on the side of cigarette packs: "Caution: Cigarette Smoking May Be Hazardous to Your Health."

1967: The Air Quality Act is passed by Congress. It doesn't have much power to enforce its goals.

1969: Cigarette advertising is banned on television and on the radio in the U.S.

1970: The Environmental Protection Agency (EPA) is established. The agency sets limits for pesticide use.

1970: President Nixon signs the Clean Air Act. It requires that the EPA set standards for pollutants that are harmful to human health and the environment (including lead, which must be phased out by the mid-1980s).

1971: President Richard Nixon signs the Lead-Based Paint Poisoning Prevention Act.

1973: The Consumer Product Safety Commission is created. Its role, according to Congress, is to "protect the public against unreasonable risks of injuries and deaths associated with consumer products."

1977: The FDA requires that U.S. cosmetics manufacturers list ingredients on product labels.

1982: Tamper-resistant packaging regulations are issued by FDA in the wake of the Tylenol poisonings that occurred earlier that year, when seven people died from capsules that had been laced with cyanide (see p. 139). The Federal Anti-Tampering Act, passed in 1983, makes it a crime to tamper with packaged consumer products.

1990: An amendment to the Clean Air Act bans lead from gasoline, effective 1995.

2002: Levels of lead found in children between one and five years old are found to have been reduced by more than 80 percent between 1976 and 1999.

RESOURCE GUIDE

PLACES TO VISIT IN PERSON OR ONLINE:

Alnwick Garden, Alnwick Castle, Alnwick, England

Includes as many as a hundred varieties of toxic plants (alnwickgarden.com)

American Association of Poison Control Centers

This is the main website representing the United States' fifty-five poison centers, which help prevent and treat poison exposures. According to their website: "Poison centers offer free, confidential medical advice 24 hours a day, seven days a week through the Poison Help line at 1-800-222-1222. This service provides a primary resource for poisoning information and helps reduce costly hospital visits through in-home treatment." (aapcc.org)

American Museum of Natural History, New York

Check out the exhibition *The Power of Poison* online at amnh.org/exhibitions/the-power -of-poison.

Centers for Disease Control and Prevention

Includes tips on preventing unintentional poisoning (cdc.gov/homeandrecreationalsafety /poisoning/index.html)

International Spy Museum, Washington, D.C.

A museum exploring the craft, practice, history, and contemporary role of espionage; includes a model of the Bulgarian ricin umbrella (spymuseum.org)

Museum of Science and Industry, Chicago

Check out the museum's crime lab. Solve a crime at the museum using fingerprint analysis, chromatography, white-powder analysis, and microscopy techniques. (msichicago.org)

Mütter Museum of the College of Physicians of Philadelphia

A museum that has a collection of weird medical stuff from the nineteenth century, including a display about poisons (muttermuseum.org)

National Museum of Health and Medicine, Silver Spring, Maryland

Established during the Civil War as a center for the collection of specimens for research in military medicine and surgery (medicalmuseum.mil)

DOCUMENTARY (TRUE) FILMS

"A Grave Threat," in "The Clean Room," *Cosmos: A Spacetime Odyssey,* season 1, episode 6 (April 21, 2014)
The story of Clair Patterson and lead (channel.nationalgeographic.com/cosmos-a-spacetime-odyssey/videos/a-grave-threat)

The Poisoner's Handbook, PBS
From 2013, a film about the history of toxicology in the United States, based on Deborah Blum's bestselling book (pbs.org/wgbh/americanexperience/films/poisoners/player)

Prohibition, PBS
Ken Burns and Lynn Novick's three-part documentary from 2011 (pbs.org/kenburns/prohibition)

POISON IN POPULAR MOVIES

Arsenic and Old Lace (1944): A dark comedy about a man who discovers that his two sweet elderly aunts have been poisoning boarders.

D.O.A. (1950): A man is told he's been poisoned and, with only a few days to live, he tries to find out who has killed him.

The Hunger Games (2012): A dystopian science-fiction story about a girl who must fight to the death to survive (warning: PG-13). Includes poison in the plot.

The Princess Bride (1987): A modern fairy-tale adventure that features a famous poison scene.

Romeo and Juliet (many versions): Based on Shakespeare's famous tragedy and featuring a famous poison scene, the story of two young lovers (spoiler alert) does not end happily.

The Sixth Sense (1999): A movie about a boy who communicates with spirits, including those who have died from poisoning (warning: it's a little scary).

Snow White and the Seven Dwarfs (1937): The animated Disney film featuring a poisoned apple.

POISON IN LITERATURE

There are many, many examples. Here are some of my favorites:

Agatha Christie stories: try *The Pale Horse, Appointment with Death, A Pocket Full of Rye, Death in the Clouds, Three Act Tragedy*

Sir Arthur Conan Doyle, Sherlock Holmes stories: try *A Study in Scarlet,* "The Adventure of the Devil's Foot"

Dorothy L. Sayers, *Strong Poison*

Shakespeare: try *Hamlet, Romeo and Juliet, Antony and Cleopatra, A Midsummer Night's Dream*

More Recent Books for Younger Readers

Julie Berry, *The Scandalous Sisterhood of Prickwillow Place*

Suzanne Collins, *The Hunger Games*

Gareth Hinds's Shakespeare adaptations

Robin LaFevers, *Grave Mercy*

J. K. Rowling, Harry Potter series

Louis Sachar, *Holes*

Kevin Sands, *The Blackthorn Key*

Anne Ursu, *The Real Boy*

Nancy Werlin, *And Then There Were Four*

Bridget Zinn, *Poison*

SOURCE NOTES

The source of each quotation or special fact in this book is listed here. The citation indicates the first words of the quotation.

Chapter 2

11 Moisturized to Death: "Deadly medication? Bonn scientists shed light on the dark secret of Queen Hatshepsut," History of the Ancient World, http://www.historyoftheancientworld .com/2011/08/deadly-medication-bonn-scientists-shed-light-on-the-dark-secret-of-queen -hatshepsuts-flacon/

Chapter 3

20 "His legs grew cold and stiff": Plato, *Phaedo,* Translated by (trans.) Harold North Fowler, Loeb Classical Library (Cambridge: Harvard University Press, 1990), 401–3, sections 117e–118a.

26 Toxic chemicals fed to ducks: Hayes, *Principles and Methods,* 12.

27 Ancient Roman Hair and Makeup—Get the Look!: From Ovid's *The Art of Love* and Pliny the Elder's *Natural History,* as quoted in Olson, Kelly, *Dress and the Roman Woman: Self-Presentation and Society* (New York: Routledge, 2008), chapter 2, pp. 58–80.

29 "mother-in-law's poison": Ovid, quoted in A. Wallace Hayes and Claire L. Kruger, eds., *Principles and Methods of Toxicology,* 6th ed. (Boca Raton, FL: CRC Press, 2014), 14.

32 Nero . . . went on calmly eating: Tacitus, *The Annals,* 13: XV–XVII, posted by William Carey from C. D. Fisher, *Cornelii Taciti Annalium* (Oxford: 1906), thelatinlibrary.com /historians/tacitus/tacitus10.html.

33 Augustus poisoning story: Cassius Dio, Roman History 56:30, Loeb Classical Library, 9 volumes, Greek texts and facing English translation: Harvard University Press, 1914–1927. Translation by Earnest Cary. http://penelope.uchicago.edu/Thayer/E/Roman/Texts/Cassius_Dio/56*.html

Chapter 4

38 "Gather the seeds of the leeks": *"Regimen Sanitatis Salernitanum—A Salernitan Regimen of Health,"* godecookery.com/regimen/regimn12.htm.

38 "a many footed worm which rolls up in a ball": H. P. Cholmeley, ed. and trans., *John of Gaddesden and the Rosa Medicinae* (Oxford: The Clarendon Press, 1912), 49.

38 Elfsickness: Nathan Belofsky, *Strange Medicine: A Shocking History of Real Medical Practices Through the Ages* (New York: Perigree, 2013), 23.

Chapter 5

46 "the most horrible and fearfull to the nature of man": Garthine Walker, *Crime, Gender and Social Order in Early Modern England* (New York: Cambridge University Press, 2003), 144.

49 "died sodainly": Richard Hall, *The Life and Death of That Renowned John Fisher, Bishop of Rochester* (London: 1655; Ann Arbor and Oxford: Early English Books Online Text Creation Partnership, 2003), quod.lib.umich.edu/e/eebo/A45326.0001.001?view=toc.

53 That Pale Renaissance Complexion—Get the Look!: Jo Wheeler, *Renaissance Secrets: Recipes and Formulas* (London: Victoria and Albert Museum, 2009), 39.

54 "How to Remove Hair:" Caterina Sforza, *Gli Experimenti,* Jacqueline Spicer, trans., http://sites.eca.ed.ac.uk/renaissancecosmetics/cosmetics-recipes/hair.

57 "It can scarce be said": James Primerose, *Popular Errours; or, The Errours of the People in Physick, First Written in Latine by the Learned Physitian James Primrose Doctor in Physick* (London: 1651), as quoted by Paul Middleton, "Poisons, Potions, and Unicorn Horns," earlymodernmedicine.com/poisons-potions-and-unicorn-horns/.

59 "Unicorne . . . is not the proper": Ambroise Paré, *The Workes of That Famous Chirurgion Ambrose Parey Translated Out of Latine and Compared with the French,* trans. Thomas Johnson (London: 1634), 814. Ann Arbor and Oxford: Early English Books Online Text Creation Partnership, 2007.

60 "There is no keeping company with it": Cennino d'Andrea Cennini, *The Craftsman's*

Handbook: "Il Libro dell'Arte," trans. Daniel V. Thompson Jr. (New Haven: Yale University Press, 1933; repr., New York: Dover, 1954), noteaccess.com/Texts/Cennini/2.htm.

60 "Of the many painters I have known": Bernardino Ramazzini, *Diseases of Workers,* trans. Wilmer Cave Wright (New York: Hafner Publishing Company, 1964), 67.

61 poisoned by his pigments: Olga Khazan, "How Important Is Lead Poisoning to Becoming a Legendary Artist?," *Atlantic,* November 25, 2013.

Chapter 6

63 Life Expectancy: A Matter of Life and Death: Plymouth Ancestors, "Raising Children in the Early 17th Century: Demographics."

63 "dog bytes . . . lethargy . . . grief . . .": John Graunt, *Natural and Political Observations Mentioned in a Following Index, and Made upon the Bills of Mortality* (London: 1665), Echo Cultural Heritage Online, echo.mpiwg-berlin.mpg.de/ECHOdocuView?url=/permanent/echo/mpi_rostock/Graunt_1665/index.meta.

75 "for a boil'd salad" . . . "would fondly kiss and paw": Robert Beverley, *The History and Present State of Virginia, in Four Parts* (London: 1705; Chapel Hill: University of North Carolina at Chapel Hill, 2006), docsouth.unc.edu/southlit/beverley/beverley.html.

Chapter 7

81 "the natives brought fruit": Sander L. Gilman and Zhou Xun, eds., *Smoke: A Global History of Smoking* (London: Reaktion Books, 2004), 30.

82 By 1634, the English colonists . . . were producing well over a million pounds of tobacco a year. Steven Sarson, "Chesapeake Region," in *Tobacco in History and Culture: An Encyclopedia,* ed. Jordan Goodman (Detroit: Scribner, 2005), 1: 117–25, Gale Virtual Reference Library.

83 "a custome lothsome to the eye": James I, "A Counterblaste to Tobacco," laits.utexas.edu/poltheory/james/blaste/blaste.html.

84 "Comb Ye Head upwards & stroke . . .": *A Book of Phisick, Made June 1710,* 38.

87 "bruised to a perfect paste": Liza Picard, *Dr. Johnson's London: Coffee-Houses and Climbing Boys, Medicine, Toothpaste and Gin, Poverty and Press-Gangs, Freakshows and Female Education* (New York: St. Martin's, 2001), 167.

88 One man suffering from serious stomach troubles: "Case of Lead Colic from Swallowing Small Shot," *London Medical Gazette: Or, Journal of Practical Medicine,* Volume 21, 1838, 940.

Chapter 8

91 What's My Line?: Anthony S. Wohl, *Endangered Lives: Public Health in Victorian Britain* (Cambridge, MA: Harvard University Press, 1983), 265.

93 The workers' jaws: Ibid., 269.

95 the Arsenic Century: James C. Whorton, *The Arsenic Century: How Victorian Britain Was Poisoned at Home, Work, and Play* (New York: Oxford University Press, 2010).

95 "scattering a dust of poison": "The Week," *The British Medical Journal* 2, October 25, 1862, 448.

97 Death by Decor: William J. Broad, "Hair Analysis Deflates Napoleon Poisoning Theories," *The New York Times,* June 10, 2008, nytimes.com/2008/06/10/science/10napo.html?_r=0.

97 "I die before my time": Francesco Mari, Elisabetta Bertol, Vittorio Fineschi, and Steven B. Karch, "Channelling the Emperor: What Really Killed Napoleon?," *Journal of the Royal Society of Medicine* 97, no. 8 (2004): 397–99.

98 Where There's a Will: Wohl, *Endangered Lives,* 11; John Buckingham, *Bitter Nemesis: The Intimate History of Strychnine* (Boca Raton, FL: CRC Press, 2008), 88; Whorton, *The Arsenic Century,* 28; "Life-Insurance and Burial Club Murder," *The British Medical Journal* 1, no. 896 (March 2, 1878), 308–9.

102 "My Lord, there is but one deadly agent": *American Medicine* 5 (June 20, 1903), 977.

102 Van Gogh's Flower Power: Frank Browning, "Who Really Cut Off Van Gogh's Ear?," National Public Radio, May 10, 2009, npr.org/templates/story/story.php?storyId=103990820.

106 Step Right Up: Cynthia Graber, "Snake Oil Salesmen Were on to Something," *Scientific American,* November 1, 2007.

Chapter 9

113 "evil change in his physical condition": "The Man Who Is Leading the Fight for Pure Food," *The Washington Times* (Washington, DC), November 20, 1904, page 5, image 29, col. 4.

113 "Oh, here's to good old germs": "Dr. Wiley's Poison Squad Enlisted from Expert Topers," *The St. Louis Republic* (St. Louis, MO), December 6, 1903, page 12, image 40, col. 4.

117 Toxic Cocktails: Deborah Blum, *The Poisoner's Handbook: Murder and the Birth of Forensic Medicine in Jazz Age New York* (New York: Penguin, 2010), 191.

117 as many as twelve hundred people: Ibid., 157.

118 "The desire to obtain some kind of drink": "Most of our Liquor Poison, 741 Deaths in City in 1926, Norris Reports to Walker: Finds Alcohol a Menace," *The New York Times,* February 6, 1927, 1.

119 screaming in straitjackets: Blum, *Poisoner's Handbook,* 121.

120 sought medical treatment for lead poisoning: Ibid., 123.

120 One study noted: Gerald Markowitz and David Rosner, *Deceit and Denial: The Deadly Politics of Industrial Pollution* (Berkeley, CA: University of California Press, 2002), 52, 104.

121 According to the results of a recent study: Rick Nevin, "How Lead Exposure Relates to Temporal Changes in IQ, Violent Crime, and Unwed Pregnancy," *Environmental Research* 83, no. 1 (May 2000): 1–22.

121 In a study by the Centers for Disease Control and Prevention: Clean Air Act Timeline.

126 The Radium Girls: Blum, *Poisoner's Handbook,* 178–79; R. E. Rowland, *Radium in Humans: A Review of U.S. Studies* (Argonne, IL: Argonne National Laboratory, September 1994); Roger M. Macklis, "Radithor and the Era of Mild Radium Therapy," *The Journal of the American Medical Association* 264, no. 5 (1990): 614–18; personal interviews with William Lamb and Jacqueline Carroll Hanratty.

128 "harmless in every respect": See, for example, "Radithor (ca. 1928)," orau.org/ptp/collection/quackcures/radith.htm.

132 In a shrewd marketing move: Christine M. Kreiser, "LIGHTS OUT," *American History* 49, no. 6 (February 2015): 18.

134 A Taste of His Own Medicine: Michael Wines, "New Study Supports Idea Stalin Was Poisoned," *The New York Times,* March 5, 2003; Miguel A. Faria, "Stalin's Mysterious Death," *Surgical Neurology International* 2 (2011): 161, ncbi.nlm.nih.gov/pmc/articles/PMC3228382.

136 The Umbrella Murder: Colin Evans, *The Casebook of Forensic Detection: How Science Solved 100 of the World's Most Baffling Crimes* (New York: Wiley, 1996), 246–47.

Chapter 10

142 Death by Post: Edward Jay Epstein, "The Anthrax Attacks Remain Unsolved," *The Wall Street Journal,* January 24, 2010.

146 Secret Assassins: Will Storr, "How Radioactive Poison Became the Assassin's Weapon of Choice: The Mysterious Life and Brutal Death of a Russian Dissident," *Matter,* November 26, 2013, medium.com/matter/how-radioactive-poison-became-the-assassins-weapon-of-choice -6cfeae2f4b53#.1i3rshvpn.

148 Way to Glow: "Stasi's Radioactive Hold over Dissidents," *BBC News,* January 4, 2001, news.bbc.co.uk/2/hi/europe/1100317.stm.

149 Arafat's Last Days: "Q&A: Investigation into Yasser Arafat's Death," *BBC News,* December 26, 2013, bbc.com/news/world-middle-east-20512259; Deborah Blum, "The Maybe-Murder of Yasser Arafat," *Wired,* November 7, 2013, wired.com/2013/11/the-maybe-murder-of -yasser-arafat.

SELECTED BIBLIOGRAPHY

Here are some of the websites I used that you might find helpful for further research.

ncbi.nlm.nih.gov, nlm.nih.gov, and nih.gov
The websites of the National Center for Biotechnology Information, the U.S. National Library of Medicine, and the National Institutes of Health. These sites have incredible resources for the researcher of medicine or public health.

godecookery.com
A treasure trove of medieval and Renaissance recipes

lead.org.au
A global lead advice and support site

fda.gov
The website for the U.S. Food and Drug Administration

cpsc.gov
The website for the U.S. Consumer Product Safety Commission

Here's a list of some of the books and other sources I used. If you'd like to find out more about poisons and their history, these might help.

Accum, Friedrich Christian. *A Treatise on Adulterations of Food, and Culinary Poisons, Exhibiting the Fraudulent Sophistications of Bread, Beer, Wine, Spirituous Liquors, Tea, Coffee, Cream, Confectionery, Vinegar, Mustard, Pepper, Cheese, Olive Oil, Pickles, and Other Articles Employed in Domestic Economy, and Methods of Detecting Them.* London: J. Mallett, 1820.

Aldersey-Williams, Hugh. *Periodic Tales: A Cultural History of the Elements, from Arsenic to Zinc.* New York: Ecco/HarperCollins, 2012.

Bell, Gail. *Poison: A History and a Family Memoir.* New York: St. Martin's, 2002.

Bell, Suzanne. *Drugs, Poisons, and Chemistry.* New York: Facts on File, 2008.

Belofsky, Nathan. *Strange Medicine: A Shocking History of Real Medical Practices Through the Ages.* New York: Perigee, 2013.

Berenbaum, May. *Bugs in the System: Insects and Their Impact on Human Affairs.* Reading, MA: Addison-Wesley, 1995.

Blum, Deborah. *The Poisoner's Handbook: Murder and the Birth of Forensic Medicine in Jazz Age New York.* New York: Penguin, 2010.

Blyth, Alexander Wynter. *A Dictionary of Hygiène and Public Health, Comprising Sanitary Chemistry, Engineering, and Legislation, the Dietetic Value of Foods, and the Detection of Adulterations, on the Plan of the "Dictionnaire d'Hygiène Publique" of Professor Ambroise Tardieu.* London: C. Griffin, 1876.

Brandt, Allan M. *The Cigarette Century: The Rise, Fall, and Deadly Persistence of the Product That Defined America.* New York: Basic Books, 2009.

Breslaw, Elaine G. *Lotions, Potions, Pills, and Magic: Health Care in Early America.* New York: New York University Press, 2012.

Browne, G. Lathom, and C. G. Stewart. *Reports of Trials for Murder by Poisoning, by Prussic Acid, Strychnia, Antimony, Arsenic, and Aconitia: Including the Trials of Tawell, W. Palmer, Dove, Madeline Smith, Dr. Pritchard, Smethurst, and Dr. Lamson, with Chemical Introduction and Notes on the Poisons Used.* London: Stevens and Sons, 1883.

Buckingham, John. *Bitter Nemesis: The Intimate History of Strychnine.* Boca Raton, FL: CRC Press, 2008.

Burney, Ian A. *Poison, Detection, and the Victorian Imagination.* Manchester: Manchester University Press, 2006.

Carr, Donald Eaton. *The Deadly Feast of Life.* Garden City, NY: Doubleday, 1971.

Christison, Robert. *A Treatise on Poisons, in Relation to Medical Jurisprudence, Physiology, and the Practice of Physic.* Edinburgh: John Stark, 1829.

Clark, Claudia. *Radium Girls: Women and Industrial Health Reform, 1910–1935.* Chapel Hill: University of North Carolina Press, 1997.

Cloulas, Ivan. *The Borgias.* Translated by Gilda Roberts. New York: F. Watts, 1989.

Cobb, Cathy, and Monty L. Fetterolf. *The Joy of Chemistry: The Amazing Science of Familiar Things.* Amherst, NY: Prometheus, 2005.

Cohen, Elizabeth S., and Thomas V. Cohen. *Daily Life in Renaissance Italy.* Westport, CT: Greenwood, 2001.

Collard, Franck. *The Crime of Poison in the Middle Ages.* Westport, CT: Praeger, 2008.

Dupré, Ruth. "Prohibitions." In *Tobacco in History and Culture: An Encyclopedia.* Edited by Jordan Goodman. Detroit: Scribner, 2005. 2: 456–67. Gale Virtual Reference Library.

Durant, Will, and Ariel Durant. *The Age of Reason Begins: A History of European Civilization in the Period of Shakespeare, Bacon, Montaigne, Rembrandt, Galileo, and Descartes: 1558–1648.* New York: Simon and Schuster, 1961.

Emsley, John. *The Elements of Murder: A History of Poison.* New York: Oxford University Press, 2005.

Evans, Colin. *The Casebook of Forensic Detection: How Science Solved 100 of the World's Most Baffling Crimes.* New York: Wiley, 1996.

Flanders, Judith. *The Invention of Murder: How the Victorians Revelled in Death and Detection and Created Modern Crime.* New York: St. Martin's Press, 2011.

———. *The Victorian City: Everyday Life in Dickens' London.* London: Atlantic Books, 2012.

Frank, Patricia, and M. Alice Ottoboni. *The Dose Makes the Poison: A Plain-Language Guide to Toxicology.* Hoboken, NJ: Wiley, 2011.

Frieda, Leonie. *Catherine de Medici: Renaissance Queen of France.* New York: HarperCollins, 2003.

Gilman, Sander L., and Xun Zhou, editors. *Smoke: A Global History of Smoking*. London: Reaktion, 2004.

Goodwin, William. *Diaries Dated from 1785–1810*. Volume 1. Transcribed by Mrs. J. Rothery of Earl Soham, August 2001. "Goodwin 1785." Earl Soham village website. earlsoham.org/home/village-history/goodwin-s-diaries/goodwin-1785.

Gratzer, Walter. *Terrors of the Table: The Curious History of Nutrition*. New York: Oxford University Press, 2005.

Graunt, John. *Natural and Political Observations Mentioned in a Following Index, and Made upon the Bills of Mortality*. London: Max Planck Institute for the History of Science, 1665.

Gray, Theodore. *Molecules: The Elements and the Architecture of Everything*. New York: Black Dog & Leventhal, 2014.

Green, Dominic. *The Double Life of Doctor Lopez: Spies, Shakespeare and the Plot to Poison Elizabeth I*. London: Century, 2003.

Harley, John. *Old Vegetable Neurotics: Hemlock, Opium, Belladonna and Henbane*. Charleston, SC: Nabu Press, 2012.

Hayes, A. Wallace, and Claire L. Kruger. *Hayes' Principles and Methods of Toxicology*. 6th ed. Boca Raton, FL: CRC Press, 2014.

Hunter, Donald. *The Diseases of Occupations*. London: Hodder and Stoughton, 1978.

Kean, Sam. *The Disappearing Spoon and Other True Tales of Madness, Love, and the History of the World from the Periodic Table of the Elements*. New York: Little, Brown, 2010.

Le Couteur, Penny, and Jay Burreson. *Napoleon's Buttons: How 17 Molecules Changed History*. New York: Tarcher, 2004.

Levy, Joel. *Poison: An Illustrated History*. Guilford, CT: Lyons Press, 2011.

Lewis, Robert A. *Lewis' Dictionary of Toxicology*. Boca Raton, FL: CRC Press, 1996.

Macinnis, Peter. *Poisons: From Hemlock to Botox and the Killer Bean Calabar*. New York: Arcade, 2011.

Magner, Lois N. *A History of Medicine*. New York: Marcel Dekker, 1992.

Markowitz, Gerald, and David Rosner. *Deceit and Denial: The Deadly Politics of Industrial Pollution*. Berkeley: University of California Press, 2002.

Matossian, Mary Kilbourne. *Poisons of the Past: Molds, Epidemics, and History.* New Haven: Yale University Press, 1989.

Mayor, Adrienne. *Greek Fire, Poison Arrows and Scorpion Bombs: Biological and Chemical Warfare in the Ancient World.* Woodstock, NY: Overlook Duckworth, 2003.

———. *The Poison King: The Life and Legend of Mithradates, Rome's Deadliest Enemy.* Princeton, NJ: Princeton University Press, 2009.

McKeown, J. C. *A Cabinet of Roman Curiosities: Strange Tales and Surprising Facts from the World's Greatest Empire.* New York: Oxford University Press, 2010.

Meyer, G. J. *The Borgias: The Hidden History.* New York: Bantam Books, 2013.

Mitford, Nancy. *The Sun King.* New York: Harper & Row, 1966.

Mollenauer, Lynn Wood. *Strange Revelations: Magic, Poison, and Sacrilege in Louis XIV's France.* University Park: Penn State University Press, 2006.

Morris, Richard. *The Last Sorcerers: The Path from Alchemy to the Periodic Table.* Washington, D.C.: Joseph Henry, 2003.

Mortimer, Ian. *The Time Traveler's Guide to Medieval England: A Handbook for Visitors to the Fourteenth Century.* New York: Touchstone, 2011.

Needleman, Herbert L. "History of Lead Poisoning in the World." N.d. The Lead Group. Accessed September 15, 2014. lead.org.au/history_of_lead_poisoning_in_the_world.htm.

Nevin, Rick. "How Lead Exposure Relates to Temporal Changes in IQ, Violent Crime, and Unwed Pregnancy." *Environmental Research* 83, no. 1 (May 2000): 1–22.

Paré, Ambroise. *The Workes of That Famous Chirurgion Ambrose Parey Translated Out of Latine and Compared with the French.* Translated by Thomas Johnson. London: 1634.

Perkins, Dorothy. "Wu Chao." In *Encyclopedia of China: The Essential Reference to China, Its History and Culture.* New York: Facts on File, 1998. *Ancient and Medieval History Online.* Facts on File.

Picard, Liza. *Dr. Johnson's London: Coffee-Houses and Climbing Boys, Medicine, Toothpaste and Gin, Poverty and Press-Gangs, Freakshows and Female Education.* New York: St. Martin's, 2001.

———. *Victorian London: The Life of a City, 1840–1870.* New York: St. Martin's, 2005.

Pomet, Pierre. *A Compleat History of Druggs.* London: 1737.

Porta, Giambattista della. *Natural Magick by John Baptista Porta, a Neapolitane.* Rare Book and Collections Division, Library of Congress. Transcribed from 1658 English Editon, Printed for Thomas Young and Samual Speed, at the Three Pigeons, and at the Angel in St Paul's Church-yard.

Porter, Roy. *Blood & Guts: A Short History of Medicine.* New York: W. W. Norton, 2003.

Ramazzini, Bernardino. *Diseases of Workers.* Translated by Wilmer Cave Wright. New York: Hafner Publishing Company, 1964.

Retief, Francois P., and Louise Cilliers. "Poisons, Poisoning, and Poisoners in Rome." *Medicina Antiqua.* Accessed June 30, 2014. ucl.ac.uk/~ucgajpd/medicina%20antiqua /sa_poisons.html.

Roach, Mary. *Gulp: Adventures on the Alimentary Canal.* New York: W. W. Norton, 2013.

Robinson, Tony. *The Worst Jobs in History: Two Thousand Years of Miserable Employment.* London: Pan Books, 2005.

Roueché, Berton. *The Medical Detectives.* New York: Plume, 1991.

Rubin, Stanley. *Medieval English Medicine.* Newton Abbot, UK: David & Charles, 1974.

Rupp, Rebecca. *How Carrots Won the Trojan War: Curious (but True) Stories of Common Vegetables.* North Adams, MA: Storey, 2011.

Sarson, Steven. "Chesapeake Region." In *Tobacco in History and Culture: An Encyclopedia.* Edited by Jordan Goodman. Detroit: Scribner, 2005. Volume 1. Gale Virtual Reference Library.

Stevens, Serita, and Anne Bannon. *Book of Poisons: A Guide for Writers.* Cincinnati: Writer's Digest Books, 2007.

Stone, Trevor, and Gail Darlington. *Pills, Potions, and Poisons.* Oxford: Oxford Univerity Press, 2000.

Stripp, Richard A. *The Forensic Aspects of Poisons.* New York: Chelsea House, 2007.

Stuart, David. *Dangerous Garden: The Quest for Plants to Change Our Lives.* Cambridge, MA: Harvard University Press, 2004.

Tacitus. *The Annals.* 13: XV–XVII. thelatinlibrary.com/historians/tacitus/tacitus10.html.

Thompson, C. J. S. *Poisons and Poisoners, with Historical Accounts of Some Famous Mysteries in Ancient and Modern Times.* London: H. Shaylor, 1931.

Tuchman, Barbara W. *A Distant Mirror: The Calamitous 14th Century.* New York: Ballantine Books, 1978.

Walker, Kenneth. *The Story of Medicine.* New York: Oxford University Press, 1955.

Wheeler, Jo. *Renaissance Secrets: Recipes and Formulas.* London: Victoria and Albert Museum, 2009.

Whorton, James C. *The Arsenic Century: How Victorian Britain Was Poisoned at Home, Work, and Play.* New York: Oxford University Press, 2010.

Williams, Guy. *The Age of Agony: The Art of Healing, c. 1700–1800.* Chicago: Academy Chicago Publishers, 1975.

Wohl, Anthony S. *Endangered Lives: Public Health in Victorian Britain.* Cambridge, MA: Harvard University Press, 1983.

I consulted the following periodicals:

American Journal of Public Health
Archives of Pathology and Laboratory Medicine
The Atlantic
The British Medical Journal (now known as *BMJ*)
Environmental Research
Indiana Magazine of History
International Journal of Scientific and Engineering Research
Journal of the American Medical Association
The Lancet
London Medical and Surgical Journal
London Medical Gazette
Los Angeles Times
The Musical Quarterly
The New Yorker
The New York Times
Science
Scientific American
The Wall Street Journal

PICTURE CREDITS

Credits preceded by the initials LC are from the Library of Congress Prints & Photographs Division. Credits with the initials WC are from Wikimedia Commons. Credits with the initials WL are from the Wellcome Library, London.

Chapter 1

p. 1, WC; p. 2, Ronald Grant Archive/Mary Evans Picture Library; p. 3, courtesy of the Getty's Open Content Program; p. 4 top, WL; p. 4 bottom, WL; p. 6 top, charobnica/Shutterstock; p. 6 bottom, wacpan/Shutterstock; p. 7 top left, Dionisvera/Shutterstock; p. 7 top right, Winiki/Shutterstock; p. 7 bottom, Designua/Shutterstock

Chapter 2

p. 9, Malibu Productions/The Kobal Collection; p. 11, Anagoria, via WC; p. 12, Grishankov/Shutterstock; p. 14 top, WC; p. 14 bottom, CEphoto, Uwe Aranas via WC; p. 16, WC

Chapter 3

p. 18 top, WC; p. 18 bottom, courtesy of the Getty's Open Content Program; p. 19, WL; p. 20, WC; p. 22, WC; p. 23, Marques/Shutterstock, p. 25, WC; p. 26, Mary Evans Picture Library; p. 27, Sailko via WC; p. 28, Mary Evans Picture Library; p. 30, WL; p. 31, MrArifnajafov via WC; p. 33, WC

Chapter 4

p. 34, WC; p. 35, Mary Evans Picture Library; p. 38, WC; p. 39, WL; p. 40, WC; p. 41, Asram via WC; p. 42, WL; p. 43, WC; p. 44, WC

Chapter 5

p. 45, WC; p. 46, WL; p. 47 left, Mary Evans Picture Library, p. 47 right, WC; p. 48, WL;

p. 49, parmoht hongtong/Shutterstock; p. 50, WL; p. 51, WL; p. 52, WL; p. 53, WC; p. 55, WC; p. 56 top, WL; p. 56 bottom, WL; p. 57, WL; p. 58, New York Public Library Digital Collections; p. 59, WL; p. 60, WC

Chapter 6
p. 65, WL; p. 66, WC; p. 69 left, WL; p. 69 right, Eric Isselee/Shutterstock; p. 70 left, WC; p. 70 right, WC; p. 73, Mary Evans Picture Library; p. 76, WC; p. 77, Science Photo Library; p. 78, WL; p. 79, WC

Chapter 7
p. 80, WL; p. 81, WL; p. 82 top, WL; p. 82 bottom, WL; p. 84, WC; p. 87, Aleksandar Grozdanovski/Shutterstock; p. 88, WL; p. 89 top, WC; p. 89 bottom, WC

Chapter 8
p. 90, LC-USZC4-1584; p. 91, LC-USZ62-23757; p. 92, Victorian Picture Library; p. 93, WL; p. 94, Morphart Creation/Shutterstock; p. 95, WL; p. 96, WL; p. 97, WC; p. 98, WL; p. 99, author's collection; p. 100, Museum of the History of Science, Mo Costandi via Flickr; p. 101, National Institute of Health; p. 103, WC; p. 104, WL; p. 105 top, History of Medicine (NLM); p. 105 bottom, courtesy of Scott Irvin; p. 106 top, WC; p. 106 bottom, History of Medicine (NLM); p. 108, LC-USZ62-63285; p. 109, author's collection; p. 110 top, author's collection; p. 110 bottom, LC-USF34- 032264-D; p. 111, author's collection

Chapter 9
p. 113, FDA/United States Government Work via Flickr; p. 114 top, WC; p. 114 bottom, WL; p. 115, WC; p. 116, LC-USZ62-123257; p. 117, LC-DIG-ds-00150; p. 119, author's collection; p. 120, author's collection; p. 122 top, courtesy of the Archives, California Institute of Technology; p. 122 bottom, courtesy of the Archives, California Institute of Technology; p. 123 top, LC: HAER MI-355-4; p. 123 bottom, WC; p. 126, courtesy of Ross Mullner; p. 127, WC; p. 128, © Theodore Gray; p. 129, FDA via WC; p. 130, FDA via Flickr; p. 132, The RAMC Muniment Collection in the care of the Wellcome Library, Wellcome Images; p. 133, © Noah Scalin; p. 134, LC-USW33-019081-C; p. 135, Warren K. Leffler, via WC; p. 137 top, courtesy of the International Spy Museum; p. 137 bottom, Nancy Wong via WC; p. 139 top, SpeedKingz/Shutterstock; p. 139 bottom, toon studio/Shutterstock; p. 140, The Asahi Shimbun/Getty Images

Chapter 10
p. 143, Alex Wong/Getty Images; p. 145 left, George Bridges/AFP/Getty Images; p. 145 right, Maxim Marmur/AFP/Getty Images; p. 146, courtesy of Jeanette Johnson; p. 147, NATASJA WEITSZ/Getty Images; p. 148, Prof. Quatermass via WC; p. 149, Tibor Végh via WC; p. 150, by the U.S. Food and Drug Administration, via WC; p. 151, Martin Lisner/Shutterstock

INDEX

Page numbers in **boldface** refer to illustrations.